KT-372-896

017

The Manufacturing Guides

Graphics
and Packaging
Production

ST 022691

CORNWALL COLLEGE

Rob Thompson
Photography by Martin Thompson

The Manufacturing Guides

Graphics and Packaging Production

Thames & Hudson

Learning Services
Cornwall College St Austell

Class   741.6028 THO
Barcode   STO22691
Date   04/12   Centre   Zone C

Contents

Part One

Forming and Construction

Page 2, clockwise from top left: blow molded plastic packaging; laser engraved acrylic; spot varnish; letterpress type.

First published in the United Kingdom in 2012 by Thames & Hudson Ltd, 181A High Holborn, London WC1V 7QX

Copyright © 2012 Rob Thompson and Martin Thompson

Designed by Christopher Perkins

All Rights Reserved. No part of this publication may be reproduced or transmitted in any form or by any means, electronic or mechanical, including photocopy, recording or any other information storage and retrieval system, without prior permission in writing from the publisher.

British Library Cataloguing-in-Publication Data
A catalogue record for this book is available from the British Library

ISBN 978-0-500-28988-4

Printed and bound in China on behalf of Latitude Press

To find out about all our publications, please visit www.thamesandhudson.com. There you can subscribe to our e-newsletter, browse or download our current catalogue, and buy any titles that are in print.

How to use this book

This guidebook is intended to be a source of inspiration for those involved in the process of designing packaging and graphics. Low-volume and mass-production processes utilized in the production of packaging are featured. Many printing processes are discussed, including those used to decorate paper and packaging, as well as more specialist techniques employed to decorate entire products. The case studies demonstrate the scope for creativity within the confines of graphics and packaging production and the process illustrations highlight some of the technical considerations.

How to use the processes sections

Each process begins with an introduction and a brief outline of the key reasons why it may be selected. The description focuses on the conventional application of each technology. It is up to the designer to challenge established ways of working where feasible.

The book is divided into three parts (colour coded for ease of reference): forming and construction (blue), graphics production (orange) and finishing techniques (yellow).

The technical illustrations show the inner workings of the technology. These principles are fundamental and define the technical constraints of the tools, equipment and typical set up of a workshop. Each technique within

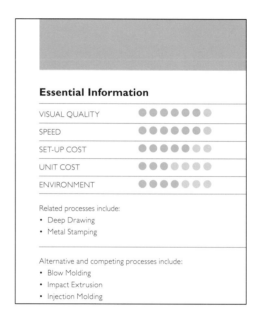

Essential Information

VISUAL QUALITY	● ● ● ● ● ● ● ○ ○ ○
SPEED	● ● ● ● ● ○ ○ ○ ○ ○
SET-UP COST	● ● ● ● ● ● ○ ○ ○ ○
UNIT COST	● ● ● ● ● ● ○ ○ ○ ○
ENVIRONMENT	● ● ● ● ○ ○ ○ ○ ○ ○

Related processes include:
• Deep Drawing
• Metal Stamping

Alternative and competing processes include:
• Blow Molding
• Impact Extrusion
• Injection Molding

Essential information
A rough guide to five key features of each process to help inform designers and aid decision-making.

a process is individually explored and explained in technical terms: for instance, paper printing, textile printing and screen-making within screen printing, or extrusion, injection and injection stretch techniques within blow molding.

How to use the essential information panels

In addition, each opening page includes a detailed essential information panel. This defines comparable values for the five key features of each process – visual quality, speed, set-up cost, unit cost and environmental

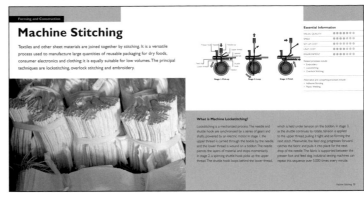

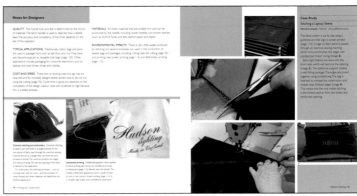

Processes and case studies Each manufacturing technology is described in detail, with at least one technical illustration and case study featuring a leading manufacturer or design studio. This example demonstrates machine stitching, which is used to produce reusable cloth bags and packaging.

impact. The scoring system is relative, with zero points the lowest and seven points the highest. The application and context of use will affect these values, but they are intended as a rough guide to help inform designers and aid decision-making.

Similar processes are often referred to by different names. For example, decal printing is used to describe transfer printing ceramics with a dye sublimation process. Within the ceramic production industry it is also referred to as bat printing or simply transfer printing.

How to use the case studies

The real-life case studies feature factories from around the world. They demonstrate some of the most innovative technologies as well as established processes that are used to make and decorate everyday products and packaging. Each of these processes is utilized in the production of well-known packaging, graphics and artwork.

The processes are covered by a step-by-step description and analysis of the key stages. The principal attributes of each technology are described in detail and some of the extended qualities, such as scale and material scope, are outlined where necessary.

Photographs of the geometry, detail, colour and surface finish are used to show the many opportunities

that each process has to offer. Leading examples demonstrate what the finished article looks like to the consumer.

Relevant links between the processes, such as forming and finishing operations, are highlighted in the text. It is essential that designers are aware of the wide range of manufacturing opportunities at their disposal. This information provides a well-informed starting point for further focused investigation, which is essential in enabling designers to harness the full potential of each manufacturing technology.

Introduction

This book features a wide range of innovative techniques used to manufacture packaging and graphics and is intended to help designers get smart about materials and manufacturing. The many factories and workshops included here are a source of inspiration. The designer dictates the crossover between packaging and graphics and this book offers insight into both areas independently.

All types of packaging are featured, including drink cans produced in the millions (see metal press forming, page 42), batch production of cotton bags (see machine stitching, page 72) and special edition wooden boxes (see wood joinery, page 68). Mass-production techniques such as machine glassblowing (page 28), blow molding (page 34) and paper pulp molding (page 20) have strict design requirements. In addition, packaging manufactured in high volumes has to be engineered so that the process is extremely reliable and efficient. Other processes, such as die cutting (page 76) and machine stitching, are more versatile and suitable for low to high volumes.

All types of graphic production techniques are discussed, including etching, engraving and printing. Long-established processes for applying graphics, such as letterpress (page 112) and screen printing (page 116), have changed very little over the years and

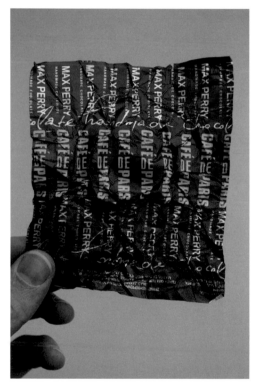

Chocolate wrapper
The striking colour of this packaging for Max Perry handmade chocolates is achieved by printing directly onto metal foil using a clear rather than an opaque basecoat. The aluminium is visible through the ink, providing a bright, reflective and metallic backdrop.

rely on skilled craftsmen who possess an in-depth knowledge of inks and substrates. In contrast, modern printing technologies, such as offset lithography (page 124), flexography (page 130, see also above), rotogravure (page 134) and digital printing (page 138), are rapidly evolving. The quality, speed and environmental impact are steadily improving. The case studies demonstrate the current state of technology and have been supplied by leading manufacturers, designers and artists. They give designers the fundamental knowledge to understand, explore and make the most of all types of packaging and graphic production techniques.

Knowledge about materials and processes

The knowledge imparted in this book is valuable for any designer developing products for manufacture. Packaging and graphics undergo a process of development so that they can be realized in production. The ability to decode and understand how things are made helps to inspire new projects, as well as to highlight potential improvements. In addition, this book provides information that will help designers ensure that their ideas do not fail for technical reasons.

Creatively combining processes and re-appropriating technologies will lead to new product experiences for the consumer. One-off, high value and special edition projects provide the greatest creative freedom for designers. For example, computer-guided processes such as laser cutting (page 104) are not limited by physical tooling. They are also versatile processes, which means that they are suitable for profiling as well as adding decoration (see above right).

Yauatcha bag This unique and distinctive packaging design by MadeThought for Yauatcha, a dim sum teahouse in London, combines die cutting (the profile), laser cutting (the decorative pattern) and foil blocking (the silver logo).

Materials and processes impact on the perception consumers have of a product, package or artwork. There is a rich choice and it is up to the designer to select the most appropriate and compelling technologies for the production of their work.

Packaging design

Packaging should protect its contents, provide relevant information for the consumer, differentiate the product from the competition, communicate the brand's values and be cost effective. Combining all these elements seamlessly and avoiding an over complex design is very challenging.

Successful packaging designers learn to be aware of all types of manufacturing and materials at their disposal. As a result, packaging solutions often combine a range of processes (see above), which

Gu Yue Long Shan Chinese rice wine Packaging plays a significant part in the overall enjoyment of products. The packaging for Gu Yue Long Shan Chinese rice wine represents luxury, quality and craftsmanship, with the use of wood, ceramic and fine printing. These qualities transfer to the contents in the mind of the consumer.

Forming techniques In many cases a package is formed in a single process. This is usually the most cost effective option and includes injection molding (page 52), EPS molding (page 24) and blow molding (page 34). There may be direct competition between processes – for example, EPS molding, injection molding, vacuum forming (page 56) and paper pulp molding (page 20) can be used for identical applications. In such cases the choice of material will have a significant impact on process selection. For example, EPS molding is only suitable for forming foamed polystyrene (PS), and paper pulp molding is limited to fibrous natural materials. By contrast, injection molding and vacuum forming are used to form a wide range of plastics and so can provide various additional functions such as rigidity and transparency.

form a strong and coherent message. This book features the principal techniques used in packaging production. Designers are not limited to these technologies: a wide range of processes, included in other titles in the *Manufacturing Guides* series, may also be considered. Packaging production is divided into forming (molding and profiling) and construction (joining).

La Vie de la Vosgienne sweets Produced by offset lithography printing onto tinplate, which is press formed, this packaging is simple, cost effective and long lasting.

Designersblock brochure Die cutting sometimes crosses over with finishing processes because it is used to cut printed materials such as this catalogue cover created by Hawaii Design for Designersblock.

Beautiful packaging does not have to incorporate unconventional manufacturing techniques or exotic materials. Metal press forming (page 42), long established in the production of tins for packaging food and drink, is used to create elegant and long-lasting packaging solutions (see opposite, right). Die cutting (page 76) is another very well-established process. It is used in the production of cartons, boxes and heavy duty cardboard boxes. In addition, it is used to profile labels and stationery, such as books and brochures (see above). Tooling costs are relatively low and therefore it is utilized in all types of applications, from hundreds of catalogues to millions of sandwich boxes.

Construction techniques Packaging is constructed using a range of techniques determined by the choice of materials. Flexible sheet materials, including paper, plastic and textile, are joined into 3D forms by folding and gluing (see carton construction, page 82), welding (see plastic welding, page 64) or by mechanical means; sheet metal is joined together by folding, gluing and welding (see metal joining, page 48); and wood is joined using conventional joinery, gluing and mechanical fixings. Typically used for mechanical purposes and hidden away, joining techniques can be exposed for decorative effect, such as comb-jointed ends on wooden wine boxes and overlock stitching on cotton bags.

Graphic design

This book covers processes used to apply graphics (i.e., text, images and patterns) to flat and 3D surfaces, directly and indirectly, for one-off and high-volume applications. Graphic designs are applied using wet ink, powder, transfer, etching, engraving or a combination of technologies. Each of these groups has very different design requirements and so is explained here to give designers a fuller understanding of the implications for their work and the creative opportunities.

Etching and engraving Graphics cut into a surface will be long lasting. The quality of the material and the skill of the craftsman will determine the quality of reproduction. Hand engraving (page 91) has changed very little since ancient times. However, the introduction of computer-guided cutting systems (see CNC engraving, page 89) has led to rapid and precise reproduction of detail in all types of materials. Similar processes include laser cutting (page 104), water jet cutting (page 100), photo etching (page 92) and abrasive blasting (page 96). Certain cutting processes are used to profile (cut out) simultaneously when applying the graphics. For example, photo etching is applied to both sides of sheet metal. Where the lines

Moschino perfume packaging Dye sublimation printing is a versatile process: it is used to print onto flat and 3D surfaces. The quality of the print reproduction is determined by ink jet printing, which is used to print the transfer medium. Alternatively, ink jet printing can be used to print directly onto flat surfaces in a process known as direct to material (DTM) (page 142).

overlap a through cut will be made because the depth of the cut is doubled.

The depth and thickness of the cut can be designed. However, the cut profile cannot always be specified: the finished effect is determined by the combination of process and material. Ink filling and gold leaf can be combined with these processes to produce high quality graphics recessed into the surface of a material.

Transfer printing Transfer printing is a versatile technique used to produce solid colour and continuous tone images on all types and shapes of materials. The blanket roll in lithography provides the 'offset', a type of transfer printing. However, offset lithography (page 124) is limited to flat sheet materials and rotationally symmetrical parts

Royal VKB nutcracker Designed by Ineke Hans for Royal VKB, the lid of the nutcracker is polyamide (PA) nylon and the clear container is polycarbonate (PC). Pad printing is used to apply ink directly onto 3D surfaces, such as the logo on this nutcracker, which would not be practical to print any other way.

(cylinders). Transfer printing lends itself to printing on 3D surfaces that are otherwise impossible or impractical to print onto directly.

Since the 1750s ceramic tableware and other products have been printed using transfers, known as bats or decals (see decal printing, page 152). The decals are produced by screen printing or offset lithography, depending on the print run required. Historically, decals were made using copperplate printing. Developments in digital printing have made it possible to print shorter runs, or even one-offs, and maintain high quality reproduction.

Dye sublimation printing (page 148) is a more recent development. Using a combination of specifically developed inks, coating technology, transfer medium, heat and pressure it is possible to coat all types of materials in all forms. This technique is already used commercially, such as for phone covers, bicycle parts and packaging (see opposite). Hydro transfer printing (page 162) is used to produce similar effects. The difference is that water is used to wrap the transfer onto the 3D form, as opposed to vacuum pressure.

Print production For centuries, paper and similar sheet materials have been printed using ink to keep records, distribute knowledge and share ideas. Printing is a fundamental part of society and the industry is well established. The processes have evolved rapidly (some more than others), techniques have been combined and computer software has greatly accelerated the production of printing plates, known as computer to plate (CTP). In principal, there are five categories of printing: relief, intaglio, planography, stencil and digital.

In relief printing the ink is applied onto raised areas of the print plate and then transferred onto the paper or other material. Letterpress (page 112) and flexography (page 130) are examples of relief printing.

Intaglio processes are the opposite: ink is collected in recesses on the print plate, which is wiped clean and then the ink is transferred onto the paper or other material such as rotogravure. Likewise, an engraved printing plate, such as the cliché used for pad printing, is a type of intaglio.

Planography is the process of applying ink from a flat surface onto paper or another material. This is possible in lithography because oily and watery liquids do not mix easily. Since the development of the transfer process, known as 'offset', in the 1870s it has become the most common commercial printing process for paper and tinplate packaging.

Stencil printing is the process of masking areas that will not be printed. Screen printing is a type of stencil printing and as a result is very versatile because many types of inks can be used. It is therefore possible to print onto different materials (see right). Risography (page 144) combines the stencil process with digital printing and demonstrates how the boundary between digital printing and conventional printing is rapidly becoming blurred as computer-guided systems are being integrated into all types of presses. Processes that are purely digital (i.e., they do not include printing plates) are ink jet (page 142) and laser printing (page 139). The advantage is that each print can be different with little or no extra cost. The quality of digital printing is very good and the speed is rapidly increasing so that for short print runs it competes with offset lithography.

Greece is for Lovers 'No Sleep Till Hades' collection
Screen printing is versatile and many different types of ink can be used and so it is possible to print the same design directly onto many different materials, such as textile and ceramic. This collection, created by Greece is for Lovers, is single colour screen printed.

Cost and the size of the print run directly impact on the selection of the process. However, the choice of colour, paper and ink are under the control of the designer.

Colour Printed colour is known as either process or spot. Process colours are cyan (blue), magenta (red), yellow and ketone (black), collectively abbreviated as CMYK. All of the colour groups can be reproduced from CMY and K is added for improved contrast and deeper blacks. Spot colours are used to match company logos or special colours, such as metallic, that cannot be achieved by mixing CMYK. Typically, a recognized

Pantone swatches
Pantone is a standard
colour system used for
specifying colours to
printers. It provides
a master against which
printed colour or coated
finishes can be checked.

standard reference system, such as Pantone (see right), is used to communicate between the designer and printer. Each colour requires a separate printing plate, so more colours means higher costs.

Most processes are not capable of printing continuous tone images – the exception is rotogravure – because colour is either printed or not. Therefore, visually continuous tone images are created using a technique known as half tone. This creates the visual effect of shades of colour. Patterns of dots, known as screens, are aligned at different angles on the printing press to avoid moiré and other undesirable visual effects. They create a rosette pattern when combined (see right, below).

Paper The print process determines what kind of paper (also referred to as stock) and ink can be used. Ultimately, it is up to the designer to balance the desired end result with cost. It is also important to consider how a design appears when printed in different ways. This is important when the applications for the design are different, such as printing adhesive labels or screen printing directly onto packs and stationery, because each process has unique qualities.

The raw ingredients of paper (recycled content, wood pulp, cotton and other fibrous materials), processing

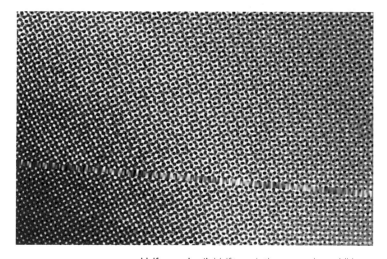

Half-tone detail Half tone is the removal or addition of printed area on the paper or other material. Due to the orientation of the screens, the clusters of dots look like rosettes. This is a close-up photograph of a print produced using offset lithography. As the concentration of dots for each colour is reduced, the visible colour changes. Half-tone dots are measured as lines per inch (lpi), not to be confused with dots per inch (dpi), which is used to measure the quality of output devices such as screens and printers.

(handmade, machine-made and calendering), sizing, fillers (such as minerals) and coating determine the quality and surface finish. The quality affects how well it can be printed on with each process. Half tones will reproduce more clearly on smooth, dense and coated paper. The spread of ink on the surface of the paper is known as dot gain and is more prevalent in absorbent, uncoated paper. The opacity of the paper will determine how much of the print can be seen on the reverse: this is known as show-through and called strike-through when the ink penetrates to the other side.

More absorbent papers soak up ink more quickly and so detail will be less well defined, but the process will be more economic because it can be run more quickly. For example, rotogravure (page 134) is used to print huge volumes at high speed and would not be cost effective if used in conjunction with papers that have slow ink penetration. Likewise, smooth paper is best for rotogravure – for speed, efficiency and good reproduction of colour – and this is why magazines are glossy.

Ink Inks are based on formulations of pigments, dyes, additives and carrier (water, oil, acrylic or natural resin).

The choice of ink is determined by the process and application. For example, it is not possible to use water-based inks with offset lithography because the process relies on water to repel the oily ink; high speed processes rely on UV-curing inks; flexography requires thinner inks than offset lithography but can be used to print water-based inks; food safe inks are required for food packaging; and pad printing requires the ink to be exactly the right viscosity so it can stick to the silicone pad only during transfer.

Speciality inks, such as food safe, metallic, thermochromatic and magnetic, have their own sets of design guidelines that must be considered in the design process and discussed with the printer. Inks may also vary according to supplier and country of origin.

Finishing

A range of processes follow after printing: folding, binding and decorating packaging and printed materials. There is an overlap between finishing and the other processes covered in this book because in many cases the finishing is carried out alongside forming, constructing and applying graphics. After all, reducing the number of processes lowers the cost of production. For example, high-volume print runs, or food cartons,

Campbell Hay wedding stationery Designed by
Campbell Hay for their friends, the Pullens, in 2009,
foil blocking is used to create high quality solid colour
and metallic graphics, which are perfectly suited
to stationery for weddings and special events. For
solid colours it is possible to colour match using
a reference such as Pantone (see page 15, above).

Versace card Embossing is used on unprinted
materials, known as blind embossing, to produce high
quality and finely detailed designs. Finishing was the
only process used in the case of this Versace card.

are produced in a single process, known as in-line.
This means that all of the operations are carried out
in sequence and without stopping.

Less common and more complex finishing processes,
such as flocking (page 176) and vacuum metalizing
(page 172), are carried out separately. Finishing
processes are typically applied to add value to
a package or print. For example, foil blocking
(page 186) is used to apply a thin metallic film
(see above, left) onto stationery, a label or a book
cover; embossing produces raised details in thin
sheet materials (see above, right), but can be used

to deboss thicker materials such as wooden boxes; and
flocking adds a soft and vividly coloured finish that feels
like velvet.

There are so many opportunities for designers to
combine processes in exciting and beautiful ways if they
understand the technologies that are available to them
and the unique qualities of each, as described in the
following chapters.

orming and Construction

Paper Pulp Molding

Molded pulp packaging is made entirely of waste materials from the paper industry. Mixed with water for molding, this natural composite material does not require adhesives, binders or other ingredients. An additive is required to improve specific qualities, such as colour, or to make the pulp waterproof.

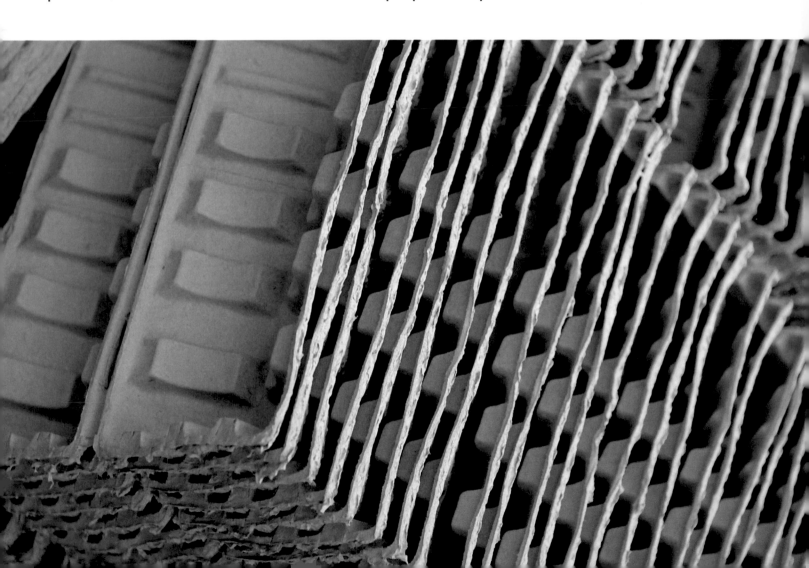

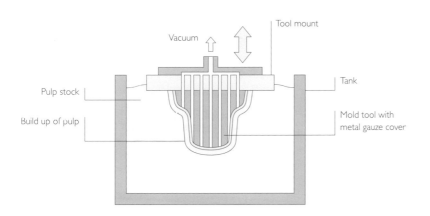

Vacuum

Tool mount

Pulp stock

Build up of pulp

Tank

Mold tool with
metal gauze cover

Essential Information

VISUAL QUALITY	●●○○○○○○
SPEED	●●●●●○○○
SET-UP COST	●●●●○○○○
UNIT COST	●●●○○○○○
ENVIRONMENT	●●●●○○○○

Related processes include:
- Air-dried
- Hot Pressing
- Wet Pressing

Alternative and competing processes include:
- Die Cutting
- EPS Molding
- Vacuum Forming

What is Paper Pulp Molding?

The mold tool is typically machined aluminium. It is covered with a fine metal gauze (see image 1, page 23) that acts like a sieve and separates the water from the wood fibres. The tool is covered with holes, which provide channels up which the water can be siphoned.

The molding is formed over the tool by a vacuum, which draws water from the pulp stock, and in doing so begins to dry out the pulp shell that forms over it.

The tool is dipped in the stock long enough for it to build up adequate wall thickness, typically 2–3 mm (0.079–0.118 in.). It is then removed from the tank and the shell is demolded and dried.

QUALITY Paper pulp is made up of natural ingredients and so by its very nature is a variable material. Even so, air-dried moldings are generally accurate to within 1 mm (0.04 in.), whereas hot-pressed moldings will be accurate to within 0.1 mm (0.004 in.). Air-dried moldings will have one smooth side (the tool side); the smoothness is improved by wet pressing or hot pressing. With such techniques, logos and fine text can be integrated.

Additives are used to improve specific properties such as making the pulp waterproof or resistant to oil.

TYPICAL APPLICATIONS The primary use of paper pulp molding is for packaging. There are a few exceptions, one of which is biodegradable flowerpots.

COST AND SPEED Tooling costs are generally low, but do depend on complexity. Wet pressing and hot pressing require additional tooling. Cycle time is rapid and labour costs are relatively low.

MATERIALS This process is specifically designed for molding paper pulp. It can be industrial or post-consumer waste, or a mixture. It is possible to mix in other fibres such as flax.

ENVIRONMENTAL IMPACTS Even though large amounts of water are required for production, this process uses 100% recycled raw material and the water is continuously recycled to reduce energy consumption. Waste produced by molding can be directly recycled and averages 3%. After use, paper pulp moldings are biodegradable or can be recycled.

Protective packaging Shipping boxes are designed to be dropped from a height of over 1 m (3.3 ft.). Carefully designed and engineered, paper pulp packaging is used to protect delicate goods, such as glass and electronic goods. Material thickness can range from 1–5 mm (0.04–0.2 in.), depending on the design needs.

Paper pulp is naturally grey or brown, depending on the stock. Typically, brown pulp is made up of craft paper and grey pulp is composed of recycled newsprint. It is possible to colour the pulp with additives.

1

2

3

4

5

Case Study

Molding Paper Pulp Packaging

Featured company Cullen Packaging
www.cullen.co.uk

The corrugated card waste produced by Cullen Packaging is raw material in the paper pulp production plant. It is mixed with water and gently pulped to avoid shortening the length of the fibres. Cullen Packaging also construct cardboard boxes (page 81).

The surface of the aluminium tools (image **1**) is covered with fine metal gauze. They are dipped in the pulp stock (image **2**), which is 1.4% paper, for around a second. The paper fibres are drawn against the surface by vacuum and collected there as the water is rapidly extracted. Fixed on a rotating arm, the tool emerges with an even coating of brown pulp (image **3**).

Water is drawn out of the pulp; it is carefully demolded onto a conveyor (image **4**) and transferred through a gas-heated oven. It is completely dry after 15 minutes or so and stacked (image **5**).

EPS Molding

EPS (expanded polystyrene) molding creates closed-cell foam that can be up to 98% air. It is lightweight, protective and insulating. Usually white, for packaging applications it is available as molded shapes, blocks that have to be cut to size or loose fill.

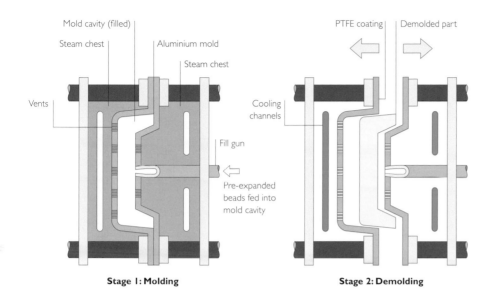

Mold cavity (filled)

Steam chest

Aluminium mold

Steam chest

Vents

Fill gun

Pre-expanded beads fed into mold cavity

PTFE coating

Demolded part

Cooling channels

Stage 1: Molding

Stage 2: Demolding

Essential Information

VISUAL QUALITY	●●●●●○○○
SPEED	●●●●●●○○
SET-UP COST	●●●●●●○○
UNIT COST	●●○○○○○○
ENVIRONMENT	●●●●●●○○

Related processes include:
- Block Molding
- Shape Molding

Alternative and competing processes include:
- Injection Molding
- Paper Pulp Molding
- Vacuum Forming
- Water Jet Cutting

What is EPS Molding?

First of all, liquid styrene monomer is subjected to a process of polymerization and combined with a blowing agent, which is usually pentane gas. This creates small granules of pre-expanded polystyrene (PS), which have a hollow, closed-cell structure. These granules expand to several times their size when exposed to steam under pressure (see image, page 26).

After maturing (stabilisation) for up to 24 hours, the granules are ready to be molded. In stage 1, steam is introduced into the mold through small vents, causing the beads to expand and bond together into a solid molding.

After steaming, excess moisture is withdrawn from the molding by vacuum.

In stage 2, the mold halves separate and the finished part is mechanically ejected. The surface of the aluminium mold is coated with polytetrafluoroethylene (PTFE), also known as DuPont Teflon, which has low surface friction to help the demolding.

QUALITY The size of the pre-expanded beads determines the density of the final product, which, in turn, affects the surface finish. The surface of the mold is replicated on the EPS, including all the signs of manufacture such as vents and the fill point.

TYPICAL APPLICATIONS EPS is used for a wide range of packaging applications, including food, drinks, white goods and consumer electronics. It is also utilized widely outside the packaging industry, such as in protective clothing, watersport products and in composite panels.

COST AND SPEED Tooling costs are moderate and mold life is long. Cycle time is around 60 minutes per part, not including the pre-expanding phase. Labour costs are relatively low.

MATERIALS PS.

ENVIRONMENTAL IMPACTS Thermoplastic scrap can be directly recycled. However, there is very little PS in EPS because it is foamed, making it more challenging to recycle after use. Pentane is a flammable gas, but is otherwise relatively harmless. Biodegradable, starch-based biopolymers can be foamed and molded into packaging and loose fill. However, at present it is not a suitable alternative to EPS for many applications and so not seen as a significant competitive threat.

Pre-expanded PS and EPS The pre-expanded PS beads on the right are already many times larger than the raw PS, which has a similar appearance to sugar. In the mold, heat and steam are used to make them expand further to produce EPS foam. In the mold cavity their growth is restricted, causing the cells to join together and form dense closed-cell foam with a smooth outer surface.

Case Study

Molding a Fish Box

Featured company Sundolitt Ltd
www.sundolitt.co.uk

In preparation, the pre-expanded EPS beads are matured in huge flexible silos (image **1**). Once the PS has been foamed it becomes very bulky, so this process is almost always carried out at the factory where it is to be molded and near to where it will be used.

In this case, the base and lid of the fish box are molded simultaneously (image **2**). The mold is green because of the PTFE coating and the vents are clearly visible on the surface of this half.

The mold halves clamp shut, the pre-expanded beads are injected into the mold and fully expanded with steam and pressure (image **3**). The finished boxes are conveyed from the mold (image **4**) and stacked by hand.

1

2

3

4

Machine Glassblowing

Compressed air and mechanical pressure form molten glass into cooled molds in mass-production glassblowing. Very precise detail can be achieved using these techniques, including screw threads and embossed logos. This is an energy intensive process, but glass is a long-lasting material and readily recycled.

| Stage 1 | Stage 2 | Stage 3 | Stage 4 | Stage 5 | Stage 6 | Finished bottle |

Essential Information

VISUAL QUALITY	●●●●●●○
SPEED	●●●●●●○
SET-UP COST	●●●●●●○
UNIT COST	●●●○○○○
ENVIRONMENT	●●●●●○○

Related processes include:
- Machine Blow and Blow
- Machine Press and Blow

Alternative and competing processes include:
- Blow Molding
- Glass Press Molding

What is Machine Blow and Blow Glassblowing?

Two different molding methods are used – either press and blow or blow and blow. The processes are essentially the same, except that the parison (pre-form) is either pressed or blown. The blow and blow technique is used for containers with a narrower neck.

In stage 1, the molten glass gob is fed into a parison mold. In stage 2, a plunger rises and presses a neck into the molten glass and in stage 3, air is injected through the mold into the formed neck.

In stage 4, the mold opens and a partially formed vessel is released and inverted through 180°. In stage 5, the bottle is transferred to the second blow mold. In stage 6, air is injected through the neck to blow the vessel into its final shape. The glass cools against the sides of the mold before it opens and releases the part.

Notes for Designers

QUALITY Glass is a material that has a high perceived value because it combines very good surface finish and decorative qualities with high strength. Certain glass materials can withstand intense heating and cooling and sudden temperature changes.

TYPICAL APPLICATIONS Glassblowing is suitable for a variety of vessels, containers and bottles, including tableware, cookware, food and pharmaceutical packaging, storage jars and tumblers.

COST AND SPEED Tooling costs are moderate. Mechanized molding cycles are extremely fast. Beatson Clark produce in excess of 15,000 glass containers every 24 hours (page 31).

MATERIALS Soda-lime glass is the most commonly used for high-volume production. It is made up of silica sand, soda ash, limestone and other additives.

ENVIRONMENTAL IMPACTS Glassblowing is energy intensive and so there have been many developments in recent years to reduce energy consumption. Despite this, glass has many beneficial qualities: glass containers can be reused many times (such as the British milk bottle and the Finnish drinks bottle), it is 100% infinitely recyclable, is made from locally sourced, readily available raw materials. Recycling 1 tonne of glass saves around 300kg (661 lbs) of carbon dioxide equivalent emissions. Once formed, it is totally inert and does not contain harmful chemicals.

500 ml (0.9 pint) beer bottle Clear glass cannot tolerate colour contamination, but amber and green glass can use a high percentage of recycled content (cullet). Beatson Clark use around 52% of cullet to make their amber glass containers and 28% for clear glass. In addition, calumite, itself a recycled material, is used to aid the refining process, enabling the glass to be melted at a lower temperature and some virgin raw materials to be replaced.

1

2

3

4

5

Case Study

Glassblowing a Beer Bottle

Featured company Beatson Clark
www.beatsonclark.co.uk

Molten glass is drawn through the furnace and conditioned (slowly cooled) to its working temperature of approximately 1150°C (2100°F). This process takes up to 24 hours. The conditioned glass flows from the bottom of the forehearth and is cut into 'gobs' (image **1**).

The gobs are fed into molds in the bottle-making machine below. The molten glass settles into the molds and the neck is formed. These freshly formed parisons (image **2**) are then inverted through 180° into the blow mold (image **3**) in tandem. The blow mold closes and the parisons are filled with compressed air, which forces the molten glass onto the surface of the cool mold. The mold opens and the fully formed bottles (image **4**) are transferred to a gas-fired lehr for annealing (image **5**).

What is Machine Press and Blow Glassblowing?

In the past, the press and blow method was limited to wide-mouthed jars. This is no longer the case and narrow neck bottles, similar to the blow and blow process, can be made in this way. In stage 1, the molten glass gob is fed into a parison mold. In stages 2 and 3, a plunger rises and presses a neck into the molten glass.

In stage 4, the mold opens and a partially formed vessel is released and inverted through 180°. In stage 5, the bottle is transferred to the blow mold. In stage 6, air is injected through the neck to blow the vessel into its final shape. The glass cools against the sides of the mold before the mold opens and the part is released.

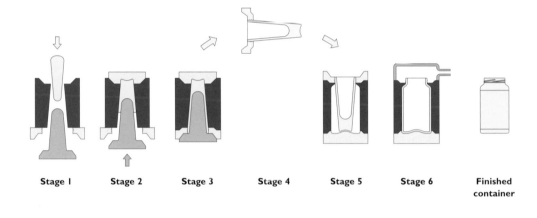

| Stage 1 | Stage 2 | Stage 3 | Stage 4 | Stage 5 | Stage 6 | Finished container |

Condiment jar Very precise detail, such as screw threads and embossed logos, can be achieved. The tolerances are fine and repeatability is good. However, designers must be very considerate about stress concentrations in the final product. Smoothing out the shape as much as possible will reduce stress, although tight radii can be achieved where necessary. Problems may occur in screw cap features, for example. Designers generally work to draft angles of 5°, but this is not a problem when working with round and elliptical shapes. It is advised that parts are kept symmetrical and that the neck is centralized because the product has to fit into conventional production, filling and labelling lines.

1

2

3

4

5

Case Study

Glassblowing a Condiment Jar

Featured company Beatson Clark
www.beatsonclark.co.uk

Just as with the machine blow and blow method (page 29), molten glass is prepared in a furnace and fed into the molds. However, in the first stage of molding, the parison is formed by a plunger instead of compressed air. The formed parison (image 1) is transferred through 180° to the blowing mold where it takes the place of blown jars as they are ejected (image 2).

After blowing, the mold halves separate and the hot jar is removed by a robotic arm (images 3 and 4). The jars are fed by conveyor belt through the annealing lehr to remove any stress build-up. A second surface treatment is added at the 'cold end' of the lehr to improve the product's resistance to scratching and scuffing. Every container is then subject to rigorous inspections (image 5), including sidewall and base scans, pressure tests, bore tests and the checking of the flatness of the sealing surface.

Blow Molding

Blow molding is used to mass produce thin-walled packaging containers for products such as soft drinks, cosmetics and medicine. Features such as handles, screw necks and surface texture can be integrated into the molding process. The neck does not have to be vertical or tubular.

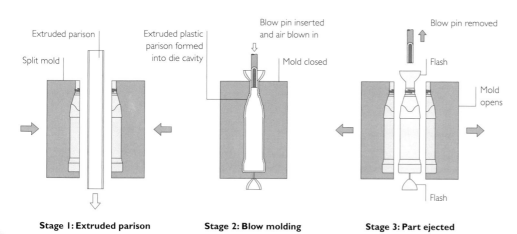

Stage 1: Extruded parison   Stage 2: Blow molding   Stage 3: Part ejected

Labels in figure:
- Extruded parison
- Split mold
- Extruded plastic parison formed into die cavity
- Blow pin inserted and air blown in
- Mold closed
- Blow pin removed
- Flash
- Mold opens
- Flash

Essential Information

VISUAL QUALITY	●●●●●○○
SPEED	●●●●●○○
SET-UP COST	●●●●○○○
UNIT COST	●●○○○○○
ENVIRONMENT	●●●●○○○

Related processes include:
- Extrusion Blow Molding (EBM)
- Injection Blow Molding (IBM)
- Injection Stretch Blow Molding (ISBM)

Alternative and competing processes include:
- Glassblowing
- Injection Molding
- Vacuum Forming

What is Extrusion Blow Molding?

In stage 1, a length of extruded plastic, known as a parison, is continuously fed from above into the mold by an extrusion machine. In stage 2, the two sides of the mold close around the parison once it has reached the correct length. Air is blown in through a blow pin, forcing it to take the shape of the mold. The hot polymer solidifies as it makes contact with the cold metal. In stage 3, when the part is sufficiently cool, the mold opens and the part is ejected. The container is deflashed using a profiled trimmer.

Notes for Designers

QUALITY The surface finish is of a very high standard for all of these processes. The injection blow molding (IBM) and injection stretch blow molding (ISBM) technologies have the additional advantage of precise control over neck details, wall thickness and weight.

TYPICAL APPLICATIONS Blow molding is used to form packaging for a wide range of products, including food and drinks, cosmetics and toiletries, medicine and chemicals.

COST AND SPEED Tooling costs are moderate to high. Extrusion blow molding (EBM) is the least expensive, the tooling for IBM typically costs twice as much and ISBM is the most expensive. Cycle time is very rapid. Labour costs are low as production is automated.

MATERIALS All thermoplastics can be shaped using blow molding, but certain materials are more suited to each of the different technologies. Typical materials used in the EBM process include polypropylene (PP), polyethylene (PE), polyethylene terephthalate (PET) and polyvinyl chloride (PVC), while the IBM process is suitable for PP and high-density PE among other materials. Typical materials for the ISBM process include PE and PET.

ENVIRONMENTAL IMPACTS All thermoplastic scrap can be directly recycled. Process scrap is recycled in-house. Post-consumer waste can also be recycled and turned into new products.

Milk container EBM is suitable for complex designs with integrated features such as the handle in this low-density polyethylene (LDPE) milk packaging. EBM is used mainly in the medical, chemical, veterinary and consumer industries to produce intravenous containers, medicine bottles and vials, and consumer packaging. Sizes range from 3 ml to 220 litres (0.005–387 pints).

1

Featured company Polimoon Packaging
www.polimoon.com

The extrusion process is continuous and produces a parison with an even wall thickness (image **1**), which is suspended between the two halves of a split mold. The mold clamps around the parison to form a seal and the parison is cut to length (image **2**). A blow rod is then inserted into the neck, and air is blown into the mold at 8 bar (116 psi), forcing the plastic to take the shape of the mold. The molds separate to reveal the blown part with the blow rods still inserted (image **3**). The rods retract and the part is deflashed with a profiled trimmer (image **4**). The finished parts (image **5**) are pressure tested prior to filling, capping and labelling (page 168).

3

2

4

5

What is Injection Blow Molding (IBM)?

The IBM process is based on a rotary table that transfers the parts to each stage in the process. In stage 1, a pre-form is injection molded over a core rod with finished neck details. The pre-form and core rod are transferred through 120° to the blowing station. In stage 2, air is blown into the pre-form, forcing the parison to take the shape of the mold. In stage 3, after sufficient cooling, the part is rotated through 120° and stripped from the core rod complete. No trimming or deflashing is needed.

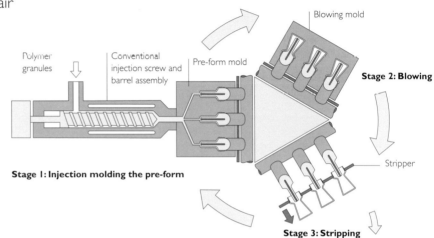

Blowing mold

Polymer granules

Conventional injection screw and barrel assembly

Pre-form mold

Stage 2: Blowing

Stripper

Stage 1: Injection molding the pre-form

Stage 3: Stripping

Stage 4: Final product

Plastic drink cans IBM is utilized in the manufacture of high volumes of consumer packaging, such as these colourful plastic drink cans. Examples of medical packaging include medicine bottles, tablet and diagnostic bottles and vials. Typical materials used include PP, PE, PET and PVC.

Case Study

Injection Blow Molding a Deodorant Bottle

Featured company Polimoon Packaging
www.polimoon.com

The polished core rods are prepared so the pre-forms can be injection molded onto them (image **1**). Each core rod is inserted into a split mold and hot molten white PP is molded onto it. The neck is fully formed (image **2**). The parts are rotated through 120° and are inserted into the blowing mold. Air is blown in through the core rod and the plastic is forced to take the shape of the mold cavity (image **3**). The parts are stripped from the core rods (image **4**) and the distinctive deodorant bottle profile can now be recognized.

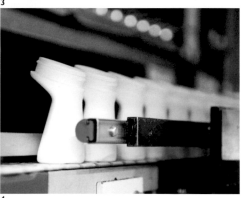

1

2

3

4

What is Injection Stretch Blow Molding (ISBM)?

In stage 1, the ISBM process uses the same technique as IBM, in that the pre-form is injection molded over a core rod. In stage 2, however, with ISBM the core rod is removed and replaced by a stretch rod. The pre-form is inserted into the blow mold, which is clamped shut.

In stage 3, air is blown in through the stretch rod, which simultaneously orientates the pre-form longitudinally. In stage 4, the mold opens and the parts are stripped from the stretch rod.

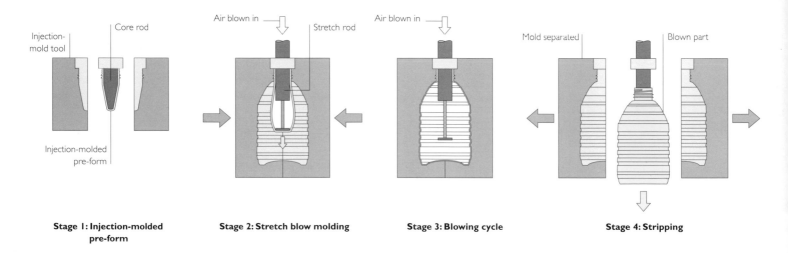

Stage 1: Injection-molded pre-form

Stage 2: Stretch blow molding

Stage 3: Blowing cycle

Stage 4: Stripping

Sei water bottle ISBM is utilized in the production of high quality packaging and is the process of choice for many drinks bottles such as this Sei water bottle. The injection cycle ensures very accurate neck finishes and the stretch cycle gives superior mechanical properties. The plastic bottle is an exact replica of the inside surface of the mold and so logos and other details can be integrated.

Case Study

Injection Stretch Blow Molding
a Chemical Container

Featured company Polimoon Packaging
www.polimoon.com

The pre-form is injection molded (image **1**) and the thin-walled parts are transferred to the blow molds (image **2**). The molds close around the pre-form and it is simultaneously stretched longitudinally and blown to form the container. The two halves of the mold separate, the containers are stripped from the stretch rod (image **3**) and do not require any trimming. The bottles are individually pressure tested (image **4**) and a cap is fitted over the injection-molded neck.

1

2

3

4

Metal Press Forming

Shaped metal packaging, such as for selling and storing food and drink, is formed by pressing sheet metal between a punch and die. Shallow parts are formed by stamping and very deep profiles can be formed using progressive dies in a process known as deep drawing.

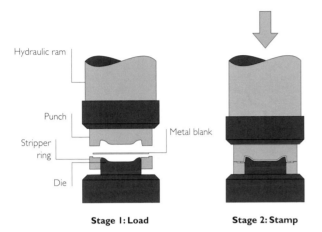

Hydraulic ram

Punch

Stripper ring

Metal blank

Die

Stage 1: Load   **Stage 2: Stamp**   **Stage 3: Strip**

Essential Information

VISUAL QUALITY	●●●●●●○
SPEED	●●●●●●○
SET-UP COST	●●●●●●○
UNIT COST	●●●○○○○
ENVIRONMENT	●●●●○○○

Related processes include:
• Deep Drawing
• Metal Stamping

Alternative and competing processes include:
• Blow Molding
• Impact Extrusion
• Injection Molding
• Metal Spinning
• Vacuum Forming

What is Metal Stamping?

Metal stamping is carried out on a punch press. The punch and die (matched tooling) are dedicated and generally carry out a single operation such as forming or punching. In operation, the metal blank is loaded onto the stripper. The punch then clamps and forms the part in a single stroke.

After forming, the stripper rises up to eject the part and it is removed. Sometimes the part is formed in a continuous strip, so many sheet-metal processes are carried out in sequence to form the part. This is the norm in very high-volume production.

Notes for Designers

QUALITY Shaped metal profiles combine the ductility and strength of metals in parts with improved rigidity and lightness. Surface finish is generally very good.

TYPICAL APPLICATIONS A wide range of everyday packaging, including cans for food and drink and flip-lid tins for mints and other sweets (see below, right). It is also utilized for high value promotional packaging such as DVD cases (see below, left).

COST AND SPEED Tooling costs are high because tools have to be extremely precise. Progressive tooling, required to produce complex or especially deep parts, increases costs considerably. Cycle time is rapid and up to 100 parts per minute can be produced.

MATERIALS Shallow profiles can be formed in malleable sheet metals such as steel, tinplate, aluminium, copper and titanium. The most suitable materials for deep profiles are steel, copper and aluminium.

ENVIRONMENTAL IMPACTS There is no heat required during this process and all scrap can be recycled. For example, using recycled material in new aluminium cans uses 95% less energy and produces 95% fewer greenhouse gas emissions. It is estimated that the aluminium used in one drink can will be used in another can only 60 days after it has been put in the recycling bin.

Bespoke packaging Used by Progress Packaging to form promotional items, such as this DVD case for Dyson, stamping is often combined with embossing (page 180) to incorporate graphics and other design details on the surface. Metal packaging is durable and perceived as high quality. In this case, the yellow colour was achieved by powder coating because printed graphics were not required.

Everyday packaging Many familiar packaging items are formed in this way, including the lids of tins used to sell and store bottles, biscuits, tea, coffee and other foods

1

Forming a Biscuit Tin Lid

Featured company Massilly www.massilly.com

The lid and base of this Fortnum & Mason biscuit tin are both formed by stamping tinplate (image **1**). The pre-printed tinplate (see offset lithography printing, page 124) is cut into strips, one lid wide. The strip is fed into the punch press (image **2**).

The metal is formed and cut out in a single stroke of the punch press (images **3** and **4**). It is a rapid process and each part is completed in a few seconds. The upper part of the tool clamps the metal in place and the lower part pushes the metal into the die forming the profile. The finished part is removed from the press (image **5**).

2

3

4

5

What is Deep Drawing?

There are many processes involved in forming and finishing aluminium two-piece cans. Deep drawing is used to form the profile of the base and walls.

In stage 1, raw sheet material is continuously fed into a deep-drawing press. A circular blank is cut out and a punch forces the metal through a draw ring and into a cup profile.

In stage 2, a thinner punch forces the metal cup through a redraw ring, which reduces the diameter of the cup to the diameter of the punch without thinning the wall section. The punch progresses downwards, forcing the metal through a series of wall-ironing rings, which reduce the wall thickness and so lengthen the cup profile.

In stage 3, the punch continues to a die that forms the base profile. Stages 2 and 3 happen in a single stroke of the punch. Every minute, each punch forms up to 1,500 complete parts. After deep drawing, the metal profile is trimmed, washed, printed, and the neck is formed and flanged. Finally, they are filled and the top is locked in place.

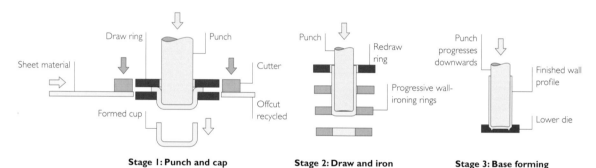

Stage 1: Punch and cap   **Stage 2: Draw and iron**   **Stage 3: Base forming**

Embossing (far left) It is possible to emboss the entire circumference of deep-drawn cans. Previously, embossing was limited to separate designs on the front and back, but now large areas can be embossed and aligned with the printed graphics.

Alumi-Tek bottle (left) Aluminium bottles are formed in the same way as aluminium two-piece cans. The difference is that the neck requires additional forming operations including applying a screw thread for the cap. In Europe and the US they are manufactured by Ball Packaging and in Japan they are made by Universal Can Corporation.

1

Deep Drawing an Aluminium Can

Featured company Ball Packaging Europe
www.ball-europe.com

All sizes of two-piece aluminium drinks cans (150–568 ml; 0.26–1 pint), such as this 500 ml (0.9 pint) Bembel with Care cider can (image **1**), are formed by deep drawing. Coils of aluminium sheet (image **2**), which weigh around 9,000 kg (20,000 pounds), are continuously fed into the deep-drawing press. Each roll will produce around 750,000 cans, depending on the size.

Formed cans emerge from the press at astonishing speed (image **3**). They are conveyed through several washing stations, which de-grease and clean the surfaces. The cans are printed using offset lithography (page 124) and spray coated with a protective varnish. Subsequent forming operations include embossing, necking and flanging. The finished cans are inspected (image **4**) and stacked on palettes. They are transferred to be filled before the stamped (page 42) lids are added.

2

3

4

Metal Joining

Metal packaging is constructed by soldering, welding, adhesive bonding or folding a tight seam. Steel tins are formed and welded or folded together, whereas aluminium cans are made from only two parts and so require little or no assembly other than capping.

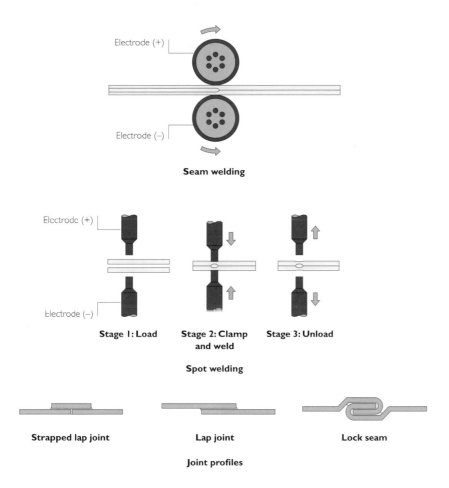

Electrode (+)

Electrode (−)

Seam welding

Electrode (+)

Electrode (−)

Stage 1: Load   **Stage 2: Clamp and weld**   **Stage 3: Unload**

Spot welding

Strapped lap joint   **Lap joint**   **Lock seam**

Joint profiles

Essential Information

VISUAL QUALITY	●●●●●●○
SPEED	●●●●●●◐
SET-UP COST	●●●●●●●
UNIT COST	●●◐●●●●
ENVIRONMENT	●●●●●●●

Related processes include:
- Adhesive Bonding
- Lock Seaming
- Mechanical Fasteners
- Resistance Welding

Alternative and competing processes include:
- Plastic Welding

What is Metal Joining?

There are two main joint profiles used to assemble sheet-metal packaging: lap joint and lock seam. Both can be soldered, welded or adhesive bonded. Alternatively, it is possible to use a lock seam without any thermal or adhesive bonding such as for dry food tins.

Hermetic seals, which are airtight and watertight, can be produced using thermal or adhesive bonding.

Resistance welding, which includes spot welding, uses a high voltage, concentrated between two electrodes, to cause the metal to heat up and coalesce. Spot welding is used for assembly operations and seam welding is used to produce a series of overlapping weld nuggets that form a hermetic seal.

Notes for Designers

QUALITY Tight seams can be formed at high speed. Welded seams will be visible on the outside of the can (see below, left) because the weld zone must be left unprinted.

TYPICAL APPLICATIONS Tins and cans for food and drink.

COST AND SPEED Tooling costs are low to moderate and most packaging conforms to a standard production line. Cycle time is very rapid: up to 2,000 parts can be formed per minute on a single production line. Labour costs are low because these processes are almost always fully automated.

MATERIALS Three-piece cans are made from tinplate, steel or aluminium, whereas two-piece cans are made from aluminium.

ENVIRONMENTAL IMPACTS Metal packaging is fully recyclable and using recycled materials reduces the environmental impact of the product. In the US around two thirds of all steel beverage packaging and half of all aluminium drink cans are recycled.

Welded seam Areas that will be welded are left uncoated to ensure a sound weld can be achieved. Welding produces a heat-affected zone (HAZ), which is clearly visible on the surface of the finished product.

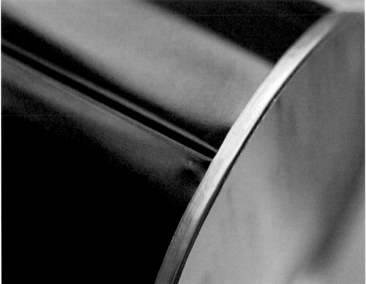

Dry seam Known as dry seams, all of the joins in tinplate packaging can be formed without adhesives, welding or soldering. In this case, the printed decoration can run right into the seam.

1

2

3

4

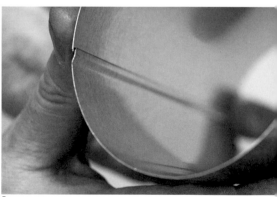

5

Case Study

Assembling a Biscuit Tin

Featured company Massilly www.massilly.com

In this case, a three-piece can is constructed by mechanically seaming the edges without any adhesive or thermal bonding (image **1**).

Sheets of pre-printed tinplate (see offset lithography printing, page 124) are cut to size (image **2**). The tube profile and lock seam of the biscuit tin are formed simultaneously and at high speed (images **3** and **4**). A strong and tight seal is formed, which is known as a 'dry' joint (image **5**) because no welding or soldering is used in the fabrication process.

The bottom of the tube is flanged and the base is mechanically seamed into it. The lid is press formed separately (page 42) and is removable. Deep-drawn aluminium cans (page 46) are only made of two pieces and do not require a seam along the length of the body.

Injection Molding

This is a rapid process used to manufacture high volumes of identical 3D parts. All types of thermoplastic materials can be shaped, including polystyrene (PS), polypropylene (PP) and polyethylene (PE). The process is utilized in the production of all types of packaging, from lids and dispensers to industrial containers.

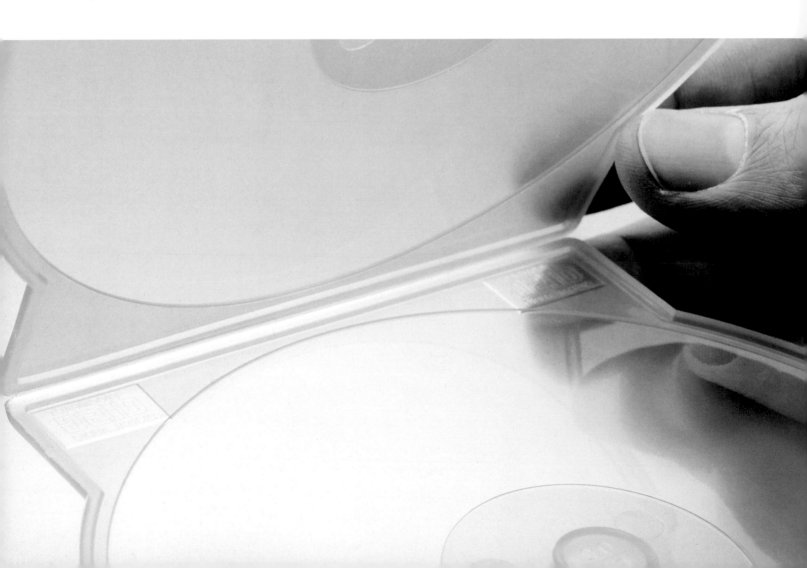

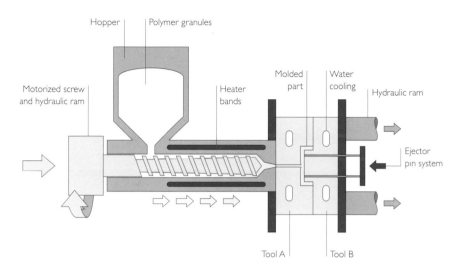

Hopper | Polymer granules

Molded part | Water cooling | Hydraulic ram

Motorized screw and hydraulic ram

Heater bands

Ejector pin system

Tool A | Tool B

Essential Information

VISUAL QUALITY	●●●●●●●○
SPEED	●●●●●●○○
SET-UP COST	●●●●●●○○
UNIT COST	●●●○○○○○
ENVIRONMENT	●●●●●○○○

Related processes include:
- Gas-assisted
- In-mold Decoration
- Twin-shot

Alternative and competing processes include:
- Blow Molding
- Die Cutting
- EPS Molding
- Paper Pulp Molding
- Vacuum Forming

What is Injection Molding?

Polymer granules are fed from the hopper into the barrel where they are simultaneously heated, mixed and moved towards the mold by the rotating action of the Archimedean screw.

The melted plastic is injected through the gate and into the die cavity at high pressure. To eject the part, the tools move apart, the cores retract and force is applied by the ejector pins to separate the part from the surface of the tool.

The least expensive injection-molding tooling consists of two halves and in this case undercuts are not feasible. However, it is possible to mold complex and undercut profiles using cores and side actions in the tool.

There are several adaptations to conventional injection molding, such as twin-shot, in-mold decoration and gas-assisted.

Notes for Designers

QUALITY The high pressure ensures good surface finish, fine reproduction of detail and, most importantly, excellent repeatability. The downside of the high pressure is that the resolidified polymer has a tendency to shrink and warp. Certain types of thermoplastic can be molded clear, with tinted colour or bright opaque colour.

TYPICAL APPLICATIONS Injection-molded products include disposable packaging, such as food tubs with snap-on lids, cosmetics and medical packaging, such as lids and dispensers, and point-of-sale displays.

COST AND SPEED Tooling costs are high and depend on the complexity of the design. Cycle time is between 30 and 60 seconds. Labour costs are relatively low. However, manual operations, such as mold preparation and demolding, increase the costs.

MATERIALS Most thermoplastic materials can be injection molded. Flexible materials include thermoplastic elastomers (TPE) and thermoplastic urethanes (TPU). The most commonly used thermoplastics include PS, PP, PE, acrylonitrile butadiene styrene (ABS) and polycarbonate (PC).

ENVIRONMENTAL IMPACTS Thermoplastic scrap can be directly recycled in this process. Up to 50% recycled material can be used in some applications, although medical and food packaging requires a higher level or has to be completely made of virgin material.

Colourful plastics (left) Molded plastic is available in a wide range of colours and opacities. The type of plastic determines what effects can be achieved. This example is PC/ABS. PS and PP are also available in vivid colours. Fluorescent dyes and brighteners are added to make the plastic appear brighter than its surroundings.

Molded detail (above) With injection molding it is possible to reproduce very good surface finish and fine details. The surface finish is determined by the surface of the tool, which can be gloss or textured. Alternatively, parts can be spray coated, printed (see dye sublimation printing, page 148) or vacuum metalized (page 172).

1

Case Study

Injection Molding a Marker Pen

Featured company Ashford Mouldings
www.ukplasticmouldings.co.uk

These Tria pen casings (image **1**) are
injection molded in black coloured PP.
The mold is made up of two halves, known
as the male tool (image **2**) and female tool.
They are machined from steel. Aluminium
alloys and copper alloys are also used in
some cases.

The mold halves are clamped together
and held tightly with hydraulic pressure
(image **3**). The polymer granules (image
4) are melted and mixed before being
injected into the die cavity. Very little black
is required to create dense colour in the
final molding. Once the die cavity has
been filled, packed and clamped, and the
polymer has resolidified, the two halves
of the mold move apart to reveal the
parts (image **5**).

The parts are ejected from the tool and
the sprues (additional parts that help the
flow of plastic from the gate) are removed.

2

3

4

5

Vacuum Forming

Thermoforming encompasses vacuum, pressure and twin-sheet forming. Vacuum forming is the most versatile and least expensive. It uses heat and pressure to shape thermoplastic materials. Packaging, signs and point-of-sale displays are commonly made in this way; it is equally suited to prototyping and mass production.

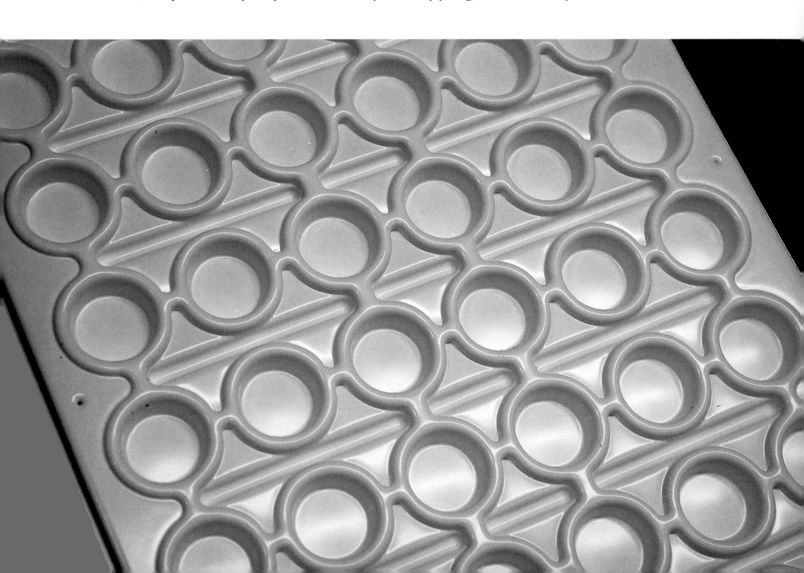

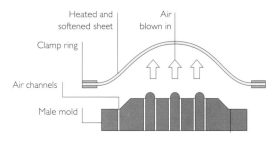

Stage 1: Pre-heated sheet

Heated and softened sheet

Clamp ring

Air blown in

Air channels

Male mold

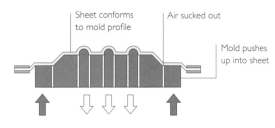

Stage 2: Vacuum forming

Sheet conforms to mold profile

Air sucked out

Mold pushes up into sheet

Essential Information

VISUAL QUALITY	●●●●●●○○
SPEED	●●●●●●○○
SET-UP COST	●●●●○○○○
UNIT COST	●●●●○○○○
ENVIRONMENT	●●●●○○○○

Related processes include:
• Pressure
• Twin-sheet

Alternative and competing processes include:
• Blow Molding
• EPS Molding
• Injection Molding
• Paper Pulp Molding

What is Vacuum Forming?

A sheet of material is heated to its softening point. For example, the forming temperature of polystyrene (PS) is 150–175°C (302–347°F). Certain materials, such as poly (methyl methacrylate) (PMMA) have a larger operating window (that is, the temperature range in which they are formable, which for PMMA is 140–190°C or 284–374°F), which makes them much easier to thermoform.

In stage 1, the softened plastic sheet is blown into a bubble, which stretches it in a uniform manner.

In stage 2, the airflow is reversed and the tool is pushed up into the sheet. A strong vacuum draws the material onto the surface of the tool to form the final shape.

So that the part can be easily removed from the mold, the vertical sides are designed with a draft angle: 2–3° taper for female molds and 5–7° for male molds. This is because the plastic will shrink and grip the mold.

Notes for Designers

QUALITY One side of a thermoformed plastic sheet comes into contact with the tool and so will have an inferior finish. However, the reverse side will be smooth and unmarked. Graphics are debossed in the surface during molding or printed onto the plastic sheet before forming.

TYPICAL APPLICATIONS Examples include packaging (trays, cups, containers, clamshells and so on), point-of-sale displays, signs and many other items as diverse as automotive interiors and boat hulls.

COST AND SPEED Tooling costs are low (very low for prototyping) to moderate, depending on the size, complexity and volume. Sheet-fed processes produce 1–8 parts per minute, whereas roll-fed machines produce hundreds of parts per minute. Sheet-fed machines are generally loaded by hand which increases labour costs.

MATERIALS Although almost all thermoplastic materials can be thermoformed, the most common are acrylonitrile butadiene styrene (ABS), polyethylene terephthalate (PET), including PETG, which is PET modified with glycol, polypropylene (PP), PS, high-impact polystyrene sheets (HIPS) and high-density polyethylene (HDPE).

ENVIRONMENTAL IMPACTS This process is only used to form thermoplastic materials, so the majority of scrap can be recycled.

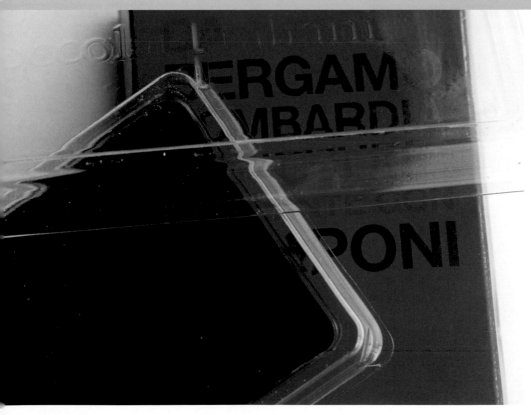

Chocolate packaging Mass-produced plastic trays used to package food are typically die cut (page 76) to size. This requires that the cutting line runs along a single plane. In other words, it cannot deviate between the horizontal and vertical axes. For low volumes and prototypes, parts are trimmed using CNC machining, which can cut along three and five axes.

1

Case Study

Vacuum Forming Packaging Trays

Featured company Global Vacuum Forming Ltd
www.gvf.co.uk

A roll of clear plastic is fed into the vacuum-forming machine (image **1**). It is heated to its softening point and clamped in place above the mold (image **2**). A strong seal is formed by the clamp, which helps to maintain air pressure once the vacuum is applied and ensure good quality moldings.

The surface of the mold is covered with tiny vent holes, which are typically 0.5–1 mm (0.02–0.04 in.) in diameter (depending on the thickness of the sheet material). They are located in places where the sheet last makes contact with the mold, such as recesses and corners, to ensure good definition of detail on the finished part.

Once the sheet is up to temperature, a small amount of air pressure is blown in before all the air is removed, pulling the sheet onto the surface of the mold (image **3**). The molded trays emerge from the vacuum-forming machine (image **4**) and are cut out, packed and shipped.

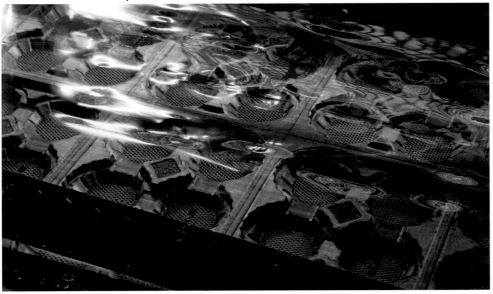

2

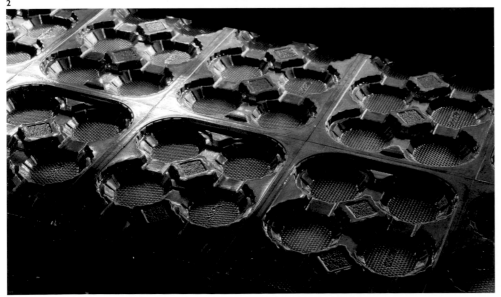

3

4

Blown Film Extrusion

Blown film extrusion, also known as tubular film extrusion, is used to produce continuous lengths of thin film. It is employed in the production of many everyday items such as plastic bags and food wrappers. It is possible to manufacture multi-layered films with various properties by co-extruding two or more polymers.

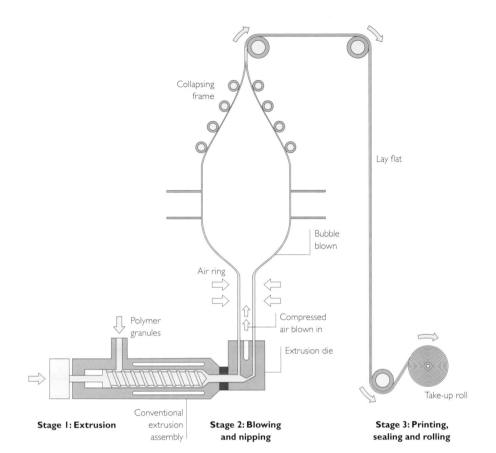

Collapsing frame

Lay flat

Bubble blown

Air ring

Compressed air blown in

Polymer granules

Extrusion die

Conventional extrusion assembly

Take-up roll

Stage 1: Extrusion　　**Stage 2: Blowing and nipping**　　**Stage 3: Printing, sealing and rolling**

Essential Information

VISUAL QUALITY	● ● ● ● ● ● ○
SPEED	● ● ● ● ● ○ ○
SET-UP COST	● ● ● ● ● ● ○
UNIT COST	● ● ● ● ● ● ●
ENVIRONMENT	● ● ● ● ○ ○ ○

Related processes include:
• Blown Film Co-extrusion

Alternative and competing processes include:
• Blow Molding

What is Blown Film Extrusion?

In stage 1, a continuous tube is formed by conventional extrusion. Molten plastic passes through the extrusion die and is simultaneously pulled upwards by the nip rolls. In stage 2, the tubular extrusion is cooled by the air ring around the outside and inflated from the inside by compressed air. As the diameter increases, the wall thickness decreases. The bubble is drawn through a series of collapsing rolls and into the nip roll as a flat sheet. By this time, the polymer has solidified and will not stick to itself.

The height of the nip rolls can be 20 m (66 ft.) and the bubble may be very small or up to 1 m (3.3 ft.) in diameter. In stage 3, the blown film is drawn through a series of rolls laid flat. Printing and sealing, to form plastic bags, for example, is carried out before the plastic film is finally wound onto the take-up spool.

QUALITY Films are strong and uniform. The combination of extrusion and blowing creates a film with good mechanical properties. Surface finish can be gloss or matt. Quality of the graphics is determined by the printing technology.

TYPICAL APPLICATIONS Blown film is used in tube form or slit into sheets. Applications include all types of plastic bags, shrink-wrap film (used to wrap food), medical packaging and agricultural sacks.

COST AND SPEED Tooling costs are moderate, but a change in colour or thickness may require the use of standard tools and so be inexpensive to set up. Printing costs are determined by the choice of process and whether it is carried out in-line or separately. In many cases, production is 24 hours per day. Labour costs are relatively low.

MATERIALS Polyethylene (PE) thermoplastics, including high density (HDPE), low density (LDPE) and linear low density (LLDPE), are the most commonly used materials. However, it is possible to form most types of thermoplastics and some biopolymers.

ENVIRONMENTAL IMPACTS Waste is created at start-up and when transitioning between colours or dimensions of film. All thermoplastic scrap can be directly recycled. Biopolymers are fully biodegradable.

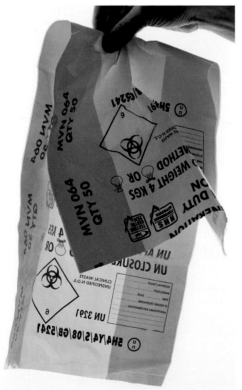

Clinical waste bag Blown film PE is the raw material used in the fabrication of a great deal of everyday packaging for applications such as transporting goods, carrier bags and plastic wrap. PE is a resilient packaging material with high resistance to puncturing and tearing. It is utilized in clinical waste bags, for example, which have to be reliable and withstand heavy use.

Case Study

Blown Film Plastic Bags

A continuous tube of extruded HDPE is inflated with compressed air as it rises upwards (image **1**). Air is blown inside through a nozzle within the extrusion die. The diameter of the tube is carefully controlled to ensure a uniform wall section. Total film thickness ranges from 20 microns (0.001 in.) to 0.3 mm (0.012 in.).

The length of tube is gradually collapsed to form a flat sheet with two layers. It continues down the side of the extrusion tower and passes through an in-line printing process at ground level (images **2** and **3**). Flexographic printing (page 130) is used because it is suitable for printing on PE. The tube is sealed, perforated, folded and wound onto a take-up spool (image **4**).

1

2

3

4

Plastic Welding

Plastic welding incorporates a range of processes used to form permanent joins in plastic materials. The joint interface is heated using ultrasonic waves, radio frequency or simply a heating element until the materials soften and mix. Pressure is applied, which encourages a strong bond to form.

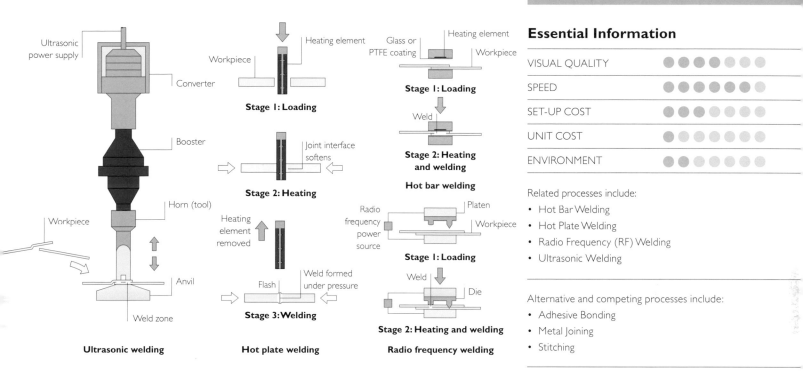

Ultrasonic welding

Ultrasonic power supply — Converter — Booster — Horn (tool) — Workpiece — Anvil — Weld zone

Hot plate welding

Heating element — Workpiece
Stage 1: Loading

Joint interface softens
Stage 2: Heating

Heating element removed — Weld formed under pressure — Flash
Stage 3: Welding

Hot bar welding

Glass or PTFE coating — Heating element — Workpiece
Stage 1: Loading

Weld
Stage 2: Heating and welding

Radio frequency welding

Radio frequency power source — Platen — Workpiece
Stage 1: Loading

Weld — Die
Stage 2: Heating and welding

Essential Information

VISUAL QUALITY	●●●●●●○
SPEED	●●●●●○○
SET-UP COST	●●●○○○○
UNIT COST	●●○○○○○
ENVIRONMENT	●●○○○○○

Related processes include:
• Hot Bar Welding
• Hot Plate Welding
• Radio Frequency (RF) Welding
• Ultrasonic Welding

Alternative and competing processes include:
• Adhesive Bonding
• Metal Joining
• Stitching

What is Plastic Welding?

Ultrasonic welding converts electrical energy into high energy vibration by means of piezoelectric discs. The horn transfers the vibrations to the workpiece. Frictional heat is generated at the joint interface, which causes the material to plasticize and mix.

Radio frequency (RF) welding, also known as high frequency or dielectric welding, uses high frequency electromagnetic energy. This process is limited to polar materials, mainly polyvinyl chloride (PVC). The electric field causes molecules in these materials to oscillate, plasticize and mix at the joint interface.

Hot bar and hot plate welding use a heating element, or profiled platen, to heat the joint interface until the materials plasticize and mix. The materials are separated from the heating elements by woven glass or a non-stick PTFE coating.

QUALITY Weld lines are visible, especially in transparent materials. Typically, the strength of joins in sheet and film is equivalent to the strength of the parent material, and hermetic seals, which do not allow liquid or gas to escape or penetrate, are possible.

TYPICAL APPLICATIONS Bags, envelopes, packets and sachets are welded.

COST AND SPEED Tooling costs are minimal for standard weld profiles. Specially designed profiles, such as for sachets that are welded and cut simultaneously, require dedicated tooling. Cycle time is rapid: ultrasonic welding is the quickest process, followed by RF, hot bar and hot plate welding. Labour costs are low to moderate.

MATERIALS Thermoplastic materials, such as PVC, TPE, PP, PE, and textiles knitted using these materials.

ENVIRONMENTAL IMPACTS No materials are added and thermoplastic materials can be recycled. Heat is generated during hot bar and hot plate welding. Ultrasonic and RF welding are an efficient use of energy: almost all of the electrical energy is converted into vibrations at the joint interface.

Liquid filled pouch Manufactured by Progress Packaging, the pouch is RF welded, filled with fake blood and then sealed. The shape is created during the first welding cycle: RF welding is used to join and profile thin-sheet materials simultaneously. The inserted label is printed by offset lithography (page 124).

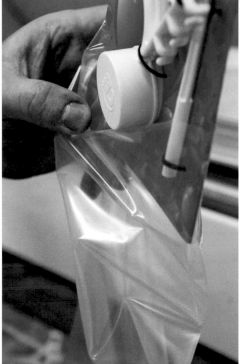

Hot Bar Welding Plastic Packaging

Featured company ENL Limited www.enl.co.uk

The card support in this packaging is offset lithography printed on one side and folded (image **1**). This is more cost effective than printing on both sides for low volumes.

The injection-molded parts are assembled and held onto the card using plastic ties. The bottom end of a plastic tube is hot bar welded and the assembly is placed inside (image **2**). The plastic is registered in the welder (image **3**) and then clamped shut (image **4**). The hot bar is concealed beneath a layer of woven glass. After a short time the bond is formed, the package is trimmed to length and the finished part is removed (image **5**).

1

2

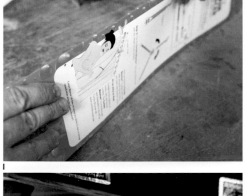

3

4

5

Wood Joinery

A combination of cabinetmaking skills and computer-guided operations are utilized in the production of wooden packaging. There is a wide choice of materials and joint types, making this a versatile process. Wood joinery is suitable for one-off, special edition and high-volume applications.

Butt joint

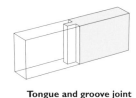

Tongue and groove joint

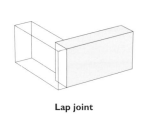

Housing joint

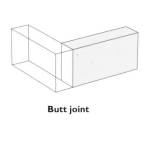

Mitre joint

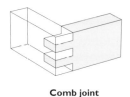

Comb joint

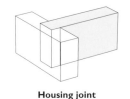

Lap joint

Essential Information

VISUAL QUALITY	●●●●●●○
SPEED	●●●●●○○
SET-UP COST	●●●●●●○
UNIT COST	●●●●●●○
ENVIRONMENT	●●●●●●○

Related processes include:
- Butt Joint
- Comb Joint
- Housing Joint
- Lap Joint
- Mitre Joint
- Tongue and Groove Joint

Alternative and competing processes include:
- CNC Machining

What is Wood Joinery?

The diagram above illustrates the most common joint types for wooden packaging. They include handmade and machine-made configurations. CNC joinery is typically produced using a router that moves along three axes, whereby x and y are horizontal and z is vertical.

There are four main types of adhesive: urea polyvinyl acetate (PVA), formaldehyde (UF), two-part epoxies and polyurethane resin (PUR). PVA and UF resins are the least expensive and most widely used. PVA is water-based and non-toxic, and excess can be cleaned with a wet cloth. PUR and two-part epoxies can be used to join wood to other materials, such as metal, plastic or ceramic, and are waterproof and suitable for exterior use. They are rigid and so restrict the movement of the joint more than PVA.

The direction of the grain at the joint interface will determine the correct type of joint. For example, the strength of a comb joint relies on end grain and would be too fragile cut across the grain.

QUALITY CNC-machined joint profiles are precise and repeatable. The choice of joint is determined by the mechanical and aesthetic requirements combined with the choice of material.

TYPICAL APPLICATIONS Wooden boxes are used as packaging for food and drink, games and special edition items.

COST AND SPEED There are not usually any tooling costs, but jigs may be required to clamp parts. Cycle time is moderate and depends on the size and complexity of the design. Labour costs are typically high due to the level of skill required.

MATERIALS All types of wood and laminate can be joined. Solid timbers include softwoods (pine, cedar, larch and douglas fir) and hardwoods (oak, ash, beech, maple, walnut and birch).

ENVIRONMENTAL IMPACTS This is a reductive process, so generates waste in operation. Dust, shavings and wood chips are often burnt to reclaim energy.

Wood has many environmental benefits, especially if it is sourced from renewable forests. Timber is biodegradable, can be reused or recycled and does not cause pollution.

Wooden packaging Wooden boxes come in all shapes and sizes. Packaging has to be cost effective and over the years a standard set of cost-efficient joint configurations has emerged. The size of joints is limited by the suitability of the workshop equipment, such as the width of the spindle cutter used to form comb joints.

1

3

2

4

Case Study

Constructing a Comb-jointed Box

Featured company Wooden Products Ltd
www.woodenproductsltd.co.uk

Lengths of pine are cut to size using
a computer-guided saw, which ensures
precise dimensions. Comb joints are cut
into the ends of each length of timber
intended for the four sides with a spindle
cutter (image **1**).

Glue is applied to all the joint surfaces
and they are assembled (image **2**). Once
sufficiently strong, the lid and base are
glued on. The sealed box is finished with
a belt sander to make all the joints flush
(image **3**).

Finally, the lid is cut from the base
(image **4**) and hinges, catches and other
metalwork are fixed in place (image **5**).
Graphics are applied by branding with
a hot embossing tool (page 180), foil
blocking (page 186), letterpress printing
(page 112) or screen printing (page 116).

5

Machine Stitching

Textiles and other sheet materials are joined together by stitching. It is a versatile process used to manufacture large quantities of reusable packaging for dry foods, consumer electronics and clothing; it is equally suitable for low volumes. The principal techniques are lockstitching, overlock stitching and embroidery.

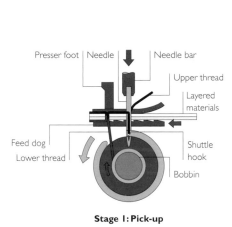

Stage 1: Pick-up

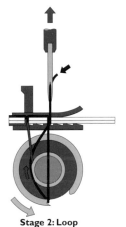

Stage 2: Loop

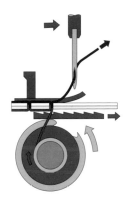

Stage 3: Finish

Labels in diagram:
Presser foot | Needle | Needle bar
Upper thread
Layered materials
Feed dog
Lower thread
Shuttle hook
Bobbin

Essential Information

VISUAL QUALITY	●●●●●●●○
SPEED	●●●●●●○○
SET-UP COST	●●●●○○○○
UNIT COST	●●●●●●○○
ENVIRONMENT	●●●●●●○○

Related processes include:
• Embroidery
• Lockstitching
• Overlock Stitching

Alternative and competing processes include:
• Adhesive Bonding
• Plastic Welding

What is Machine Lockstitching?

Lockstitching is a mechanized process. The needle and shuttle hook are synchronized by a series of gears and shafts, powered by an electric motor. In stage 1, the upper thread is carried through the textile by the needle, and the lower thread is wound on a bobbin. The needle pierces the layers of material and stops momentarily. In stage 2, a spinning shuttle hook picks up the upper thread. The shuttle hook loops behind the lower thread, which is held under tension on the bobbin. In stage 3, as the shuttle continues to rotate, tension is applied to the upper thread, pulling it tight and so forming the next stitch. Meanwhile, the feed dog progresses forward, catches the fabric and pulls it into place for the next drop of the needle. The fabric is supported between the presser foot and feed dog. Industrial sewing machines can repeat this sequence over 5,000 times every minute.

QUALITY The overall look and feel is determined by the choice of materials. The term 'handle' is used to describe how a textile feels. The accuracy and consistency of the finish depends on the skill of the operator.

TYPICAL APPLICATIONS Traditionally, cotton bags and sacks are used to package food, such as salt, flour and rice. They have also become popular as reusable tote bags (page 120). Other applications include packaging for consumer electronics such as laptops and hard drives, shoes and clothes.

COST AND SPEED There are no tooling costs, but jigs may be required and for complex designs textile panels have to be cut out using die cutting (page 76). Cycle time is good, but depends on the complexity of the design. Labour costs are moderate to high because this is a skilled process.

MATERIALS All sheet materials that are suitably thin and can be punctured by the needle, including woven textiles, non-woven textiles (such as DuPont Tyvek and felt), leather, paper and plastic.

ENVIRONMENTAL IMPACTS There is very little waste produced by stitching, but several processes are used in the production of textile bags and packages, including cutting (see die cutting, page 76) and printing (see screen printing, page 116, and letterpress printing, page 112).

Overlock stitching and embroidery Overlock stitching is used to join and finish in a single process. As the two pieces of fabric pass through the overlock sewing machine, known as a serger, they are trimmed and encased in thread. The overlock protects the edges and reduces fraying. The size and spacing of the stitch is tailored to the application.

For embroidery, the stitching technique – such as running, chain, satin or cross – and the inclusion of metal threads and other materials will determine the finished appearance.

Letterpress printing Traditionally, graphics were applied by block printing, also known as woodblock printing, or letterpress (page 112) directly onto the textile. This creates a distinctive appearance and is usually limited to one or two colours. Screen printing (page 116) is a versatile, high quality and cost-effective alternative.

1

2

3

4

Case Study

Stitching a Laptop Sleeve

Featured company Felthams www.cplfelthams.co.uk

The black cotton is cut to size using a guillotine and the logo is screen printed (page 116) (image **1**). Each piece is passed through an overlock sewing maching, which trims and finishes the edges with a protective thread casing (image **2**).

Semi-rigid battens are sewn into the short side, which will become the opening (image **3**). The additional support creates a well-fitting package. The edges are joined together using lockstitching. The bag is inverted to conceal the construction and reveals neat, finished edges (image **4**). This means that the only visible stitching is the thread used to form the folded and reinforced opening.

Die Cutting

This process is used to profile and form non-metallic sheet materials using steel knives. Using die cutting, thin-sheet materials can be cut through, kiss cut, perforated and scored with complex designs in a single operation. For high volumes it is used in-line during printing.

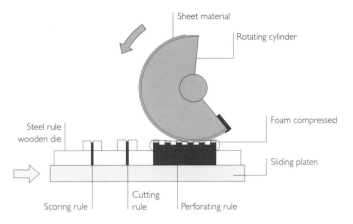

Rotary die cutting

Labels: Sheet material, Rotating cylinder, Foam compressed, Steel rule wooden die, Sliding platen, Scoring rule, Cutting rule, Perforating rule

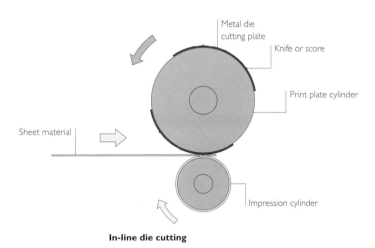

In-line die cutting

Labels: Metal die cutting plate, Knife or score, Print plate cylinder, Sheet material, Impression cylinder

Essential Information

VISUAL QUALITY	●●●●●●○○
SPEED	●●●●●●○○
SET-UP COST	●●●●○○○○
UNIT COST	●●●○○○○○
ENVIRONMENT	●●○○○○○○

Related processes include:
- In-line Die Cutting
- Platen Die Cutting
- Rotary Die Cutting

Alternative and competing processes include:
- Laser Cutting
- Punching and Blanking
- Water Jet Cutting

What is Rotary Die Cutting?

There are two main die-cutting techniques, which are distinguished by the type of production. Rotary die cutting is used to cut, score and perforate sheet materials fed into the press one by one, whereas in-line die cutting is utilized in high-volume printing, such as offset lithography (page 124), flexography (page 130) and rotogravure (page 134).

Rotary die cutting uses steel rule wooden dies as in platen die cutting (page 80). They are formed by laser cutting slots into a plywood base, in which the steel rules are securely located. In the case of in-line die cutting, the steel rules are formed in a single sheet and wrapped onto a cylinder like a printing plate.

QUALITY The tools are laser cut (page 104) and so are precise. The cutting action is between a sharp cutting rule and a steel cutting plate, and therefore results in clean, accurate cuts.

TYPICAL APPLICATIONS Die cutting is used to profile card and board for box and carton construction (see page 82). It is used to cut out labels in-line in the printing process (see flexography, page 130), and for book covers, coasters, stationery and promotional materials.

COST AND SPEED Tooling costs are low to moderate. Cycle time is rapid and automated and rotary systems may profile up to 4,000 parts per hour. Labour costs are low in automated systems.

MATERIALS Most non-metallic and non-glass sheet materials, such as paper, card, plastic, self-adhesive film, wood veneer, textile, felt and foam.

ENVIRONMENTAL IMPACTS Die cutting does produce offcuts. However, scrap can be minimized by nesting the shapes together on a sheet. Most scrap can be recycled.

Die-cut book This perfect bound (page 194) catalogue, created by Hawaii Design agency to accompany the *Decode* exhibition (2009–2010) at the Victoria and Albert Museum in London, is die cut in-line during printing which eliminates secondary processes.

Kiss-cut labels This technique is used to cut down to a specific depth and is accurate to 50 microns (0.002 in.). It is utilized to cut out self-adhesive labels, leaving the supportive backing layer intact. It is possible to kiss cut in-line, for instance, for packaging labels (see flexography, page 130). These propaganda stickers were designed by Keith Gray for Vexed Generation.

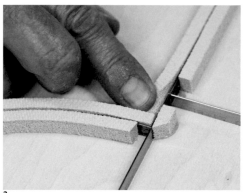

Case Study

Die Cutting and Constructing a Folder

Featured company Colchester Print Group
www.brecklandprint.com

An offset lithography printed (page 124) folder is cut out, folded and assembled (image **1**).

The steel rules are surrounded by foam (image **2**) to help eject the material after cutting and avoid it getting stuck to the blade. In this case the steel rule wooden die is loaded onto a flat bed (image **3**) that slides under a rotating cutting plate.

As one page is ejected, another is wrapped around the rotating cylinder and pressed onto the steel rule die cutter (image **4**). The pages are trimmed using a guillotine (image **5**) and assembled with adhesive.

1

2

3

4

5

What is Platen Die Cutting?

In stage 1, the sheet is loaded onto the cutting plate, which rises up to meet the die. In stage 2, the sharp steel rules cut right through the sheet material, while foam pads either side of the rules apply pressure to the sheet material to prevent it from jamming. The cutting action is instantaneous: each sheet is processed within a few seconds.

It is possible to score certain materials, such as corrugated card and plastic, using different techniques, including perforating and creasing, and by adding a ribbed strip on the cutting plate.

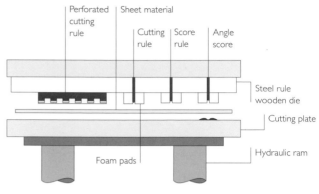

Stage 1: Load

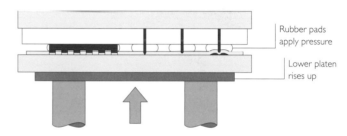

Stage 2: Die cutting

Profile and score Steel rule blades can be bent down to a 5 mm (0.2 in.) radius. Holes with a smaller diameter are cut out using a profiled punch. Sharp bends are produced by joining two steel rules together at the correct angle. All of the cutting, perforating and scoring processes are carried out in a single operation, which makes die cutting an efficient and rapid process for complex shapes and constructions.

1

2

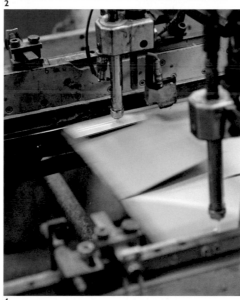

3

4

5

6

Case Study

Die Cutting and Assembling
a Crashlock Box

Featured company Cullen Packaging
www.cullen.co.uk

This crashlock cardboard box (image **1**) is produced on an automated production line at 4,000 parts per hour. It is called a 'crashlock' because the base is glued together in such a way that it unfolds as the box is opened up.

Die cutting is the most effective method for manufacturing a box like this because there are angled cuts and scores that cannot be produced by in-line printing and slotting. Very simple boxes that are scored and cut at right angles can be produced economically with rotary cutters on the end of the print line. However, as soon as there is an angle to score, such as on the base of a crashlock box, die-cutting techniques are used.

The card is die cut in an enclosed production line, after which it is fed onto the folding production line (image **2**).

The boxes are gradually assembled by the combination of levers, arms, rollers and glue dispensers (images **3–5**). The finished boxes emerge from the press, with the adhesive fully cured, flat and ready to ship (image **6**).

Case Study

Carton Construction

Featured company Alexir Packaging
www.alexir.co.uk

Cartons and packaging, such as this organic food box (image **1**), are die cut and constructed. Profiling and creasing are carried out on a platen press, which consists of a steel rule wooden die (image **2**), that presses down onto a cutting plate (image **3**).

The profiled parts are fed into a folding and gluing line. First of all, the horizontal folds are formed and glued in place (image **4**). Then, the vertical folds are made (image **5**) and the parts are pressed and stacked (image **6**).

The finished parts are kept flat for shipping (image **7**). When they are ready to be used they are unfolded and the structure is formed.

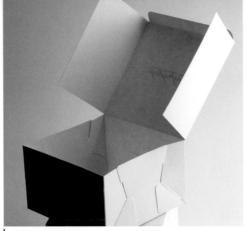

1

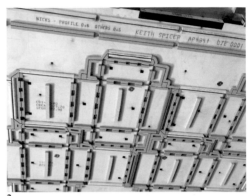

2

3

4

6

5

7

1

2

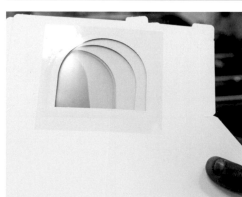
3

Case Study

Window Integration

Featured company Alexir Partnership
www.alexir.co.uk

Plastic windows are integrated into food packaging to show the contents (image **1**). This is carried out after die cutting and before construction.

The stacked sandwich box profiles (image **2**) are fed into the gluing line. The adhesive is applied by flexography (image **3**) (see flexography, page 130) and the plastic window is bonded in place (image **4**). The assembled part (image **5**) is now ready to be constructed into the finished box.

4

5

Graphics Production

2

Engraving

All types of materials can be engraved with text and graphics, including metal, plastic, wood and stone. CNC methods produce high quality results and are precise to 0.01 mm (0.0004 in.). Hand engraving has remained largely unchanged since ancient times, except that the tools are more advanced.

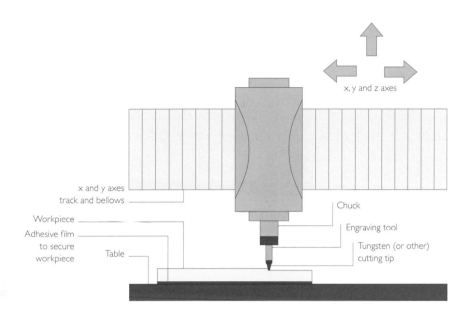

x, y and z axes

x and y axes
track and bellows

Workpiece

Adhesive film
to secure
workpiece

Table

Chuck

Engraving tool

Tungsten (or other)
cutting tip

Essential Information

VISUAL QUALITY	● ● ● ● ● ● ●
SPEED	● ● ● ○ ○ ○ ○
SET-UP COST	○ ● ● ● ● ○ ○
UNIT COST	● ● ● ● ○ ○ ○
ENVIRONMENT	● ● ○ ○ ○ ○ ○

Related processes include:
- CNC Engraving
- Hand Engraving

Alternative and competing processes include:
- Abrasive Blasting
- Laser Cutting
- Photo Etching
- Water Jet Cutting

What is CNC Engraving?

CNC engraving is a precise method for engraving 2D and 3D surfaces. The cutting speed is determined by the material and the engraving tool. Tungsten is the most commonly used material for cutting tips. It can be re-sharpened and even re-shaped several times. It is not uncommon to cut a fresh tool for each job, depending on the requirements of the design. Harder materials, such as granite, will require diamond-coated cutting bits.

The diagram above shows a 3-axis CNC machine, with all movement controlled by the track and bellows. The operating programme engraves the design either in straight lines, or following the profile of the design and creating a centrifugal pattern. The choice of cutting path depends on the shape of the engraving.

QUALITY Computer-guided processes are high quality and repeatable. A balance has to be struck between larger cutters, which will remove material more rapidly, and definition of detail. Fine lines visible in the water-clear plastic can be reduced with polishing or slower cutting speeds. The quality of hand engraving relies on the skill of the craftsman.

TYPICAL APPLICATIONS Applications include signage, trophies, artwork, precise instruments and high-end packaging.

COST AND SPEED There are no tooling costs, although tools may need to be replaced. Cycle time is moderate, but harder materials and deeper engravings require slower cutting speeds. Labour costs are moderate to high for hand techniques.

MATERIALS Materials include plastic, foam, wood, metal, stone, glass, ceramic and composite.

ENVIRONMENTAL IMPACTS All material that is removed is waste and is not normally recycled. The designer should take into account the source of the stone and method of extraction. The dust produced when carving certain stones can be harmful and so breathing apparatus is required.

Ink fill Engravings can be applied to the reverse side of clear and translucent materials. This improves the visual qualities of the engraving because the finish will be concealed beneath a smooth and uninterrupted surface layer. The visual difference is demonstrated here: the design has been layered by engraving on both the front and the back surfaces.

Filling in with colour visually eliminates any evidence of the cutting operation and has the obvious benefit of colour matching to, for example, a company logo. In addition, layers of clear material can be engraved, filled with paint and then seamlessly bonded to create the appearance of a suspended graphic element within a block of material.

CNC metal engraving Almost any rigid material is suitable for CNC engraving. However, each material requires specific cutters and it is unlikely that one factory will be capable of engraving all types of materials. Zeus! by Greece is for Lovers is made in brass; the graphics are cut into the surface using CNC engraving.

1

Case Study

CNC Engraving a Trophy

Featured company Aspect Signs & Engraving
www.aspect-signs.co.uk

The raw material, 10 mm (0.4 in.) thick poly (methyl methacrylate) (PMMA) acrylic (image **1**), is loaded onto the cutting table. The cutting tip is zeroed and synchronized with the CAD data.

Each part takes 15 minutes to machine (image **2**). A cutting tip of 0.3 mm (0.012 in.) is used because the internal radii are very tight. The engraving is carried out on the reverse side to create an immaculate gloss finish when viewed front on.

The engraved profile is filled with cellulose-based paint (image **3**). The engraving is cut just deep enough to contain the paint effectively, at 0.2 mm (0.0079 in.) thick. Multiple colours can be applied to very intricate, interweaving patterns, but this takes considerably longer. This trophy is cleaned and excess paint removed (image **4**).

2

3

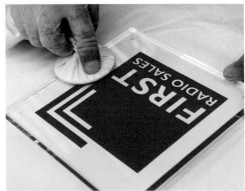

4

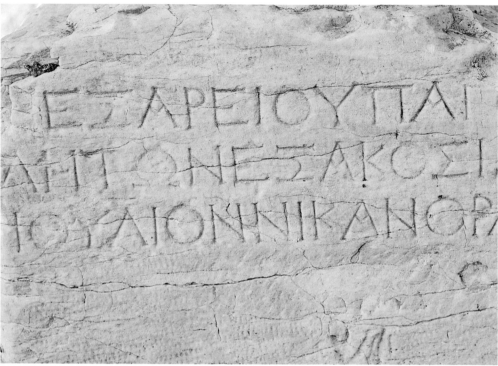

Engraved metal (above, left) All types of materials can be engraved by hand, but require different skills from stone engraving because the techniques are not the same. Metal jewelry, gun stocks and trophies are often engraved by hand and it is possible to achieve very fine details. Many types of metals can be engraved in this way including copper alloys, aluminium alloys, steel and precious metals (gold, silver, for example).

Ancient stone engraving (above, right) Stonemasonry has changed very little since this engraving was made in a piece of Pentelic marble at the Parthenon in Athens, Greece. The temple was completed in 438 BC. The engravings and carvings were originally decorated with colour, but this has since been eroded away.

Gold leaf (left) Engravings can be filled in with colour or gold leaf to make the text stand out. Gold leaf is made by hammering a nugget of gold into a very thin sheet, which is then gilded onto the engraving.

1

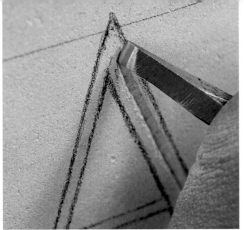

2

3

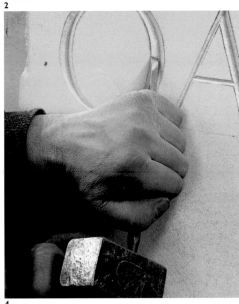

4

5

Engraving Limestone

Featured company Neil Luxton
www.neilluxton.co.uk

Cutting stone by hand requires a very skilled stonemason. Common types of stone include marble, granite, slate, limestone and sandstone. Harder materials are much more difficult to engrave and require different techniques.

First of all, the mason draws the letters to be carved in pencil (image **1**). The only guidance is the horizontal lines drawn with a straight edge.

The initial channel is roughed out by hammering a wedge-shaped chisel into the face of the stone (image **2**). The chisel has a Tungsten carbide tip, which is extremely hard. A range of chisels is used to engrave stone and the choice is determined by the type of engraving and the stone being worked (image **3**).

The mason's final lettering strokes form the edge of the engraving into a smooth profile (image **4**). Soft materials, such as limestone, can be worked relatively quickly to produce accurate and deep engravings (image **5**), whereas harder materials, such as marble and granite, will take considerably longer and require slightly different skills.

Photo Etching

Photo etching, also referred to as acid etching and wet etching, is the process of surface removal by chemical dissolution. It has a similar appearance to abrasive blasting and laser etching. The surface of the metal is masked with a resist film and unprotected areas are chemically dissolved in a uniform manner.

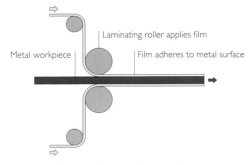

Metal workpiece

Laminating roller applies film

Film adheres to metal surface

Stage 1: Photosensitive resist

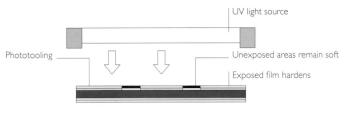

UV light source

Phototooling

Unexposed areas remain soft

Exposed film hardens

Stage 2: UV exposure

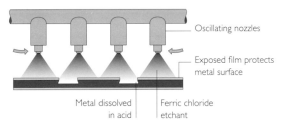

Oscillating nozzles

Exposed film protects
metal surface

Metal dissolved
in acid

Ferric chloride
etchant

Stage 3: Etching

Essential Information

VISUAL QUALITY	●●●●●●○
SPEED	●●●●●○○
SET-UP COST	●○○○○○○
UNIT COST	●●●○○○○
ENVIRONMENT	●●●●●○○

Related processes include:
- Photochemical Machining

Alternative and competing processes include:
- Abrasive Blasting
- CNC Engraving and Machining
- Laser Etching

What is Photo Etching?

In stage 1, the photosensitive polymer film is applied by dip coating or, as here, hot roll laminating. The coating is applied to both sides of the workpiece because every surface will be exposed to the chemical etching process.

In stage 2, the acetate negatives (phototooling) are applied to either side of the workpiece and the workpiece, resist and negative are exposed to UV light. The soft, unexposed photosensitive resist film is chemically developed away. This exposes the areas of the metal to be etched.

In stage 3, the metal sheet passes under a series of oscillating nozzles that apply the chemical etch. The oscillation ensures that plenty of oxygen is mixed with the acid to accelerate the process. Finally, the protective polymer film is removed.

QUALITY The etched pattern will be an exact replica of the acetate negative. The surface finish is matt and can be polished, blasted, anodized or treated using most metal finishing processes. The ductility and hardness of the metal are not affected.

TYPICAL APPLICATIONS Applications include signage, control panels, nameplates, plaques and trophies. Photo etching is also employed by jewellers and silversmiths for decorative effect.

COST AND SPEED Tooling costs are minimal. The only tooling required is a negative that can be printed directly from data, graphics software or artwork. Cycle time and labour costs are moderate. Processing multiple parts on the same sheet reduces costs considerably.

MATERIALS Most metals can be photo etched, including steel, aluminium, copper, brass and silver. Aluminium is the most rapid to etch and stainless steel takes the longest. Glass, mirror, porcelain and ceramic are also suitable, although different types of photo resist and etching chemical are required.

ENVIRONMENTAL IMPACTS The chemical used to etch the metal is one third ferric chloride. Caustic soda is used to remove spent protective film. Both of these chemicals are harmful and operators must wear protective clothing.

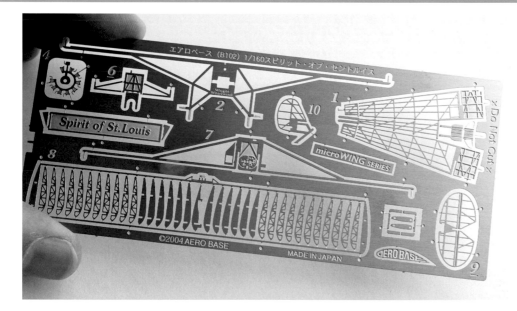

Photochemical machining Surface removal is typically 50–100 microns (0.002–0.004 in.) in a five-minute pass. Thin-sheet materials, up to 1 mm (0.04 in.) thick, can be cut as well as etched. Where the lines overlap a through cut will be made because the depth of the cut is doubled. This is known as photochemical machining.

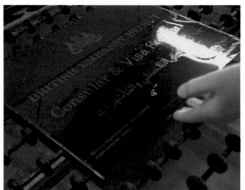

Etching Stainless Steel

Featured company Aspect Signs & Engraving
www.aspect-signs.co.uk

The process begins with a printed acetate negative. The negative is secured to one side of the workpiece and the whole assembly is placed in a light booth where it is exposed to UV light. The negative is removed (image **1**) and unexposed polymer film is washed off in a developing process (image **2**).

The workpiece now passes through the etching process, which takes up to 20 minutes (image **3**). The depth of the etch is 150 microns (0.006 in.), which is required when filling with colour. Multiple colours can be applied to very intricate patterns, but this takes considerably longer because each colour needs to dry before the next colour can be applied. Finally, excess paint is polished off (image **4**) and the plaque, which is for the British Embassy in Beirut, is finished (image **5**).

Abrasive Blasting

This is a simple process that is used to apply relief graphics on the surface of hard materials such as glass and metal. Abrasive blasting is a general term used to describe the process of surface removal by fine particles of sand, plastic and other abrasive materials.

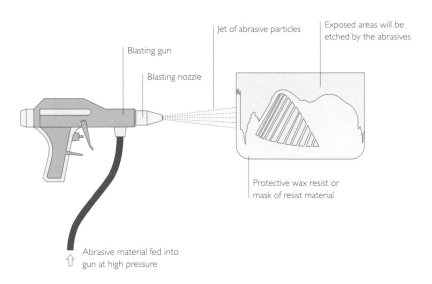

Blasting gun

Blasting nozzle

Jet of abrasive particles

Exposed areas will be
etched by the abrasives

Protective wax resist or
mask of resist material

⇧ Abrasive material fed into
gun at high pressure

Essential Information

VISUAL QUALITY	●●●●●●○
SPEED	●●●●●○○
SET-UP COST	●○○○○○○
UNIT COST	●●●○○○○
ENVIRONMENT	●●●○○○○

Related processes include:
- Bead Blasting
- Dry Etching
- Plastic Media Blasting (PMB)
- Sand Blasting
- Shot Blasting

Alternative and competing processes include:
- CNC Machining
- Laser Cutting and Engraving
- Photo Etching

What is Abrasive Blasting?

Abrasive blasting can be carried out inside a sealed booth (glove box) or a walk-in booth. Alternatively, blasting apparatus can be used on site or outdoors if the workpiece is very large or impractical to move. With most techniques, the steady stream of compressed air generally operates at pressures between 5.51 bar and 8.62 bar (80–125 psi).

The choice of abrasive material is crucial and will be affected by many factors, which include the material being etched, the depth, grade and speed of cut and economics. The abrasives are graded in much the same way as abrasive papers.

The choice of materials includes sand, glass bead, metal grit, plastic media and ground walnut and coconut shells. Certain natural materials, such as walnut shells, will not affect glass or plated material. This can be useful if, for example, the operator only wants to erode the metal part of a product made up of metal and glass.

Notes for Designers

QUALITY The surface finish is consistent and matt. Very fine details can be reproduced accurately, but the final quality can be affected by the skill of the operator or set up of the production line. The depth of texture will affect the level of transparency in clear materials by increasing light refraction.

TYPICAL APPLICATIONS Decorative applications on metal and glass include artwork, product logos, signage and trophies.

COST AND SPEED There are no tooling costs, however, masks may be required. Cycle time is good, but is slowed down by complex masking and multi-layering. Labour costs are moderate to high for manual operations and low for automated production.

MATERIALS This process is most effective for etching metal and glass surfaces, but can be used to prepare and finish the majority of materials such as wood and some polymers.

ENVIRONMENTAL IMPACTS The dust that is generated during abrasive blasting can be hazardous. Booths and cabinets can be used to contain the dust that is created. Working in a sealed booth also means that the blast materials can be reclaimed easily for reuse.

Case Study

Decorative Sand Blasting

Featured company The National Glass Centre
www.nationalglasscentre.com

The blown glass vessel being decorated here was designed by Peter Furlonger in 2005. First, the artwork is translated onto a wax resist, or mask, either by hand or by printing (image **1**), and is applied to the workpiece (image **2**). The abrasive materials cannot penetrate 'slippery' materials and bounce off, leaving the masked area untouched.

Negative etching is used to describe the process of etching the image and leaving the background intact, as is often the case with logos. This case study is an example of positive etching because the image is left intact and the background is textured.

The artist carefully etches away the unprotected areas of the workpiece in a glove box (image **3**). Once the first stage of etching is complete, specific areas of the wax resist are removed (image **4**). This will enable the artist to create a multi-layered etched image. This technique is particularly effective on this product because the coloured surface has been built up in layers: the top layer has been fired with a blowtorch to produce a metallic effect, the layer underneath is non-metallic and the base layer is clear glass.

The product is returned to the booth for the second stage of the etching process (image **5**). Finally, the wax resist and all other masking are removed so the workpiece is ready for cleaning and polishing (image **6**).

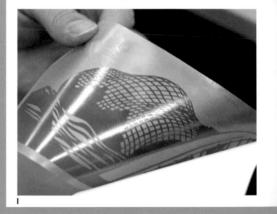
1

2

3

4

5

6

Water Jet Cutting

A supersonic jet of water, which is typically mixed with abrasives, is used to cut through almost any sheet material, including soft foam, plastic, metal and glass. It is versatile, precise and suitable for one-off and mass production. It is reasonably energy efficient and the water is continuously recycled.

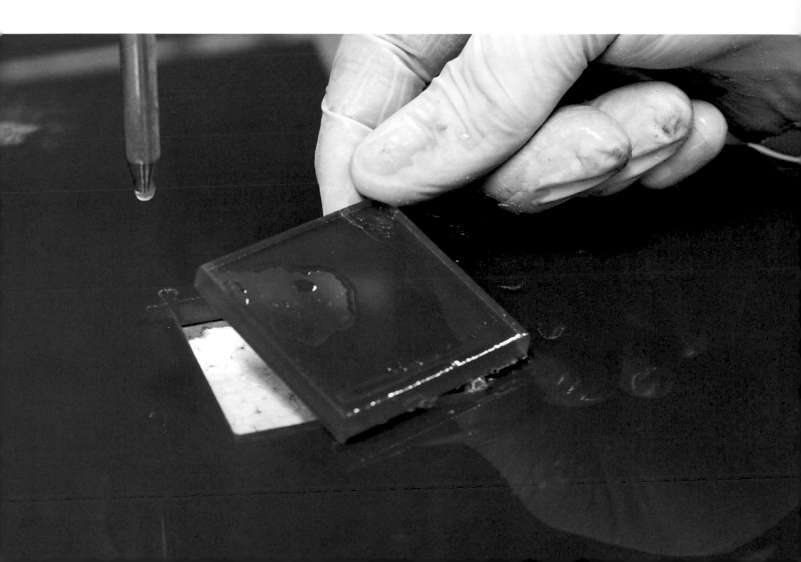

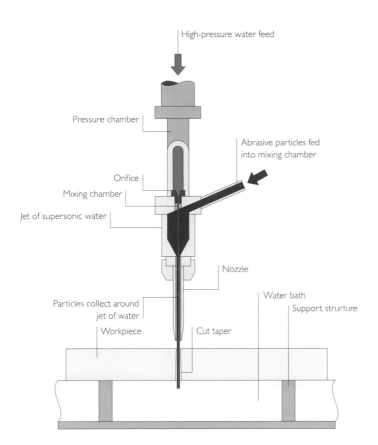

High-pressure water feed

Pressure chamber

Abrasive particles fed
into mixing chamber

Orifice

Mixing chamber

Jet of supersonic water

Nozzle

Particles collect around
jet of water

Water bath

Support structure

Workpiece

Cut taper

Essential Information

VISUAL QUALITY	●●●●●●●
SPEED	●●●●●●●
SET-UP COST	●●●●●●●
UNIT COST	●●●●●●●
ENVIRONMENT	●●●●●●●

Related processes include:
• Abrasive Water Jet Cutting

Alternative and competing processes include:
• CNC Engraving
• EPS Molding
• Laser Cutting

What is Water Jet Cutting?

Similar to CNC machining (page 87), it is possible to cut along up to 5 axes. This means angled cuts and complex geometries can be reproduced directly from CAD data.

It is carried out as either water only cutting or abrasive water jet cutting. Water is supplied to the cutting nozzle at very high pressure up to 4,000 bar (60,000 psi). It is forced through a small opening in the orifice, which measures 0.1–0.25 mm (0.004–0.009 in.) in diameter.

In abrasive water jet cutting the sharp mineral particles (often garnet) are fed into the mixing chamber and are combined with the supersonic water. The abrasive particles create a beam 1 mm (0.04 in.) in diameter, which produces the cutting action. A plain water jet can be as small as 0.75 mm (0.003 in.). The water is continuously sieved, cleaned and recycled.

Notes for Designers

QUALITY Water jet cutting is a cold process. This means that there is no discolouration along the cut edge and pre-printed or coated materials can be cut this way. It is extremely precise and for soft materials it is accurate to within 0.013 mm (0.0005 in.). The cut surface finish is matt.

TYPICAL APPLICATIONS Graphics applications include signage, trophies and exhibition pieces, for example. Soft foam packaging, profiled for added protection, is made by water jet cutting.

COST AND SPEED There are no tooling costs. Cycle time can be quite slow, but depends on the hardness and thickness of the material and the quality of cut. Labour costs are moderate.

MATERIALS Most sheet materials, including plastic, metal, ceramic, glass, wood, textiles and composites. It is possible to cut material between 0.5 mm and 100 mm (0.02–3.94 in.) thick. The hardness of the material will determine the maximum thickness. For example, polymer foam 100mm (3.94 in.) thick will cut with very little drag, but the maximum thickness for stainless steel is 60 mm (2.36 in.).

ENVIRONMENTAL IMPACTS There are no hazardous materials created in the process or dangerous vapours off-gassed. The water is usually tapped from the mains and is cleaned and recycled for continuous use.

Edge finish (left) Water jet cutting produces a matt surface finish such as on these glass cubes. Pure water jet cutting produces a much cleaner cut than abrasive systems. The sharp particles used in abrasive water jet cutting vary in size much like sandpaper (120, 80 and 50). Different grit sizes affect the quality of the surface finish: finer grit (with a higher number) is slower and produces a better quality surface finish.

Cutting wood (above) This process was originally created to machine wood. Now there are very few materials that cannot be cut in this way.

1

Water Jet Cutting Glass

Featured company Instrument Glasses
www.instrumentglasses.com

The water jet cutter is CNC, so every operation is programmed into the machine from a CAD file (image **1**). The 15 mm (0.6 in.) clear poly (methyl methacrylate) (PMMA) acrylic is loaded onto the cutting bed, which is full of water. In operation, the high velocity jet is dissipated by the bath of water below the workpiece. This water is continuously sieved, cleaned and recycled.

The cutting nozzle progresses slowly to ensure a high quality edge finish. Faster cutting speeds produce more drag, which will be visible on the edges. As it progresses, the operator inserts wedges to support the part being cut out (image **2**). The completed 'W' is removed from the sheet (image **3**) ready to be finished.

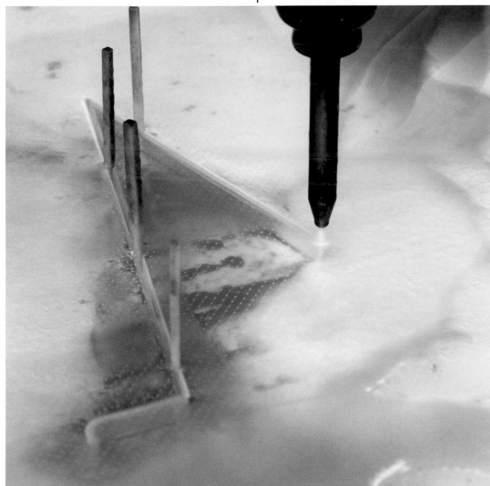

2

3

Laser Cutting

Laser cutting is a CNC process used for applications that require a high quality and precise finish. By adjusting the laser power it is possible to cut, etch, engrave and mark a variety of materials including plastic, metal, wood and leather. Known as edge-glow, tinted plastics light up along the cut edge.

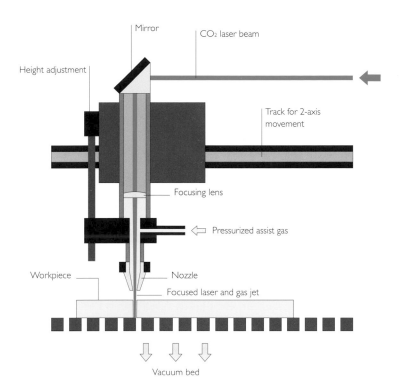

Mirror

CO_2 laser beam

Height adjustment

Track for 2-axis movement

Focusing lens

Pressurized assist gas

Workpiece

Nozzle

Focused laser and gas jet

Vacuum bed

Essential Information

VISUAL QUALITY	●●●●●●○○
SPEED	●●●●●○○○
SET-UP COST	○●●●●●●○
UNIT COST	●●●●●○○○
ENVIRONMENT	●●●●○○○○

Related processes include:
- Laser Engraving
- Laser Scoring

Alternative and competing processes include:
- CNC Machining
- Die Cutting
- Photo Etching
- Vinyl Cutting
- Water Jet Cutting

What is Laser Cutting?

CO_2 and Nd:YAG laser beams are guided to the cutting nozzle by a series of fixed mirrors. Due to their shorter wavelength, Nd:YAG laser beams can also be guided to the cutting nozzle with flexible optical fibre cores. This means that they can cut along five axes because the head is free to rotate in any direction.

The laser beam is focused through a lens to a fine spot which measures between 0.1 mm and 1 mm (0.004–0.04 in.). The high concentration beam melts or vaporizes the material on contact. The strength and depth of the laser can be controlled to produce a variety of finishes. Depending on the application, the laser can be used to cut, engrave or score (see opposite).

Edge-glow is caused by light that is picked up on the surface of the material being transmitted out through the edges. The scoring acts like an edge and so lights up in the same way. This quality is often used in signage and lighting for emphasis.

QUALITY Certain materials, such as thermoplastics, have a very high surface finish when laser cut. Laser processes produce perpendicular, smooth, clean cuts in most materials. On certain materials, such as wood (see below, left), the laser darkens the surface because the material is burnt away.

TYPICAL APPLICATIONS Applications include signs and trophies, packaging, point-of-sale, models and prototypes.

COST AND SPEED There are no tooling costs for this process. Data is transmitted directly from a CAD file to the laser cutting machine. Cycle time is rapid, but depends on material thickness. Thicker materials take considerably longer to cut.

MATERIALS This process is ideally suited to cutting thin-sheet materials down to 0.2 mm (0.0079 in.); it is possible to cut sheets up to 40 mm (1.57 in.), but thicker materials greatly reduce processing speed. Compatible materials include plastic, metal, timber, veneer, paper and card, synthetic marble, flexible magnet sheets, textile and fleece, rubber and certain types of glass and ceramic.

ENVIRONMENTAL IMPACTS Careful planning will ensure minimal waste, but it is impossible to avoid offcuts that are not suitable for reuse.

Laser engraved wood As well as laser engraving 2D surfaces, it is also possible to cut and engrave on 3D parts. Cylindrical profiles are the most straightforward because the distance between the laser and surface of the material will not change, but it is feasible to cut along almost any profile using a 5-axis machine.

Sheet acrylic The finish on acrylic is very good and does not require polishing, even for thick sheet materials. Typically, a laser cutter will have a wide range of materials in stock to reduce lead times. Sheets of acrylic come in a range of standard colours, tints and thicknesses.

1

2

Case Study

Laser Cutting

Featured company Zone Creations
www.zone-creations.co.uk

This design by Alexander Åhnebrink and Luca Cipelletti was created with Adobe Illustrator (image **1**). Laser machines use vector-based cutting systems: the lasers follow a series of lines from point to point. The files used are taken directly from CAD data, which is divided up into layers that determine the depth of each cut.

The sheet of tinted orange PMMA is cut to size (image **2**) and then transferred to the engraver. This machine etches areas of the surface away in a process known as raster engraving (image **3**). The finished part is checked (image **4**) and close inspection shows the quality of the cutting and engraving on the surface (image **5**).

5

3

4

Vinyl Cutting

This is a versatile process used to create graphics for a wide range of applications, including exhibitions, shop windows and lorry sidings. Data is transferred directly from the computer to the cutter, which is essentially an x–y plotter with a sharp blade.

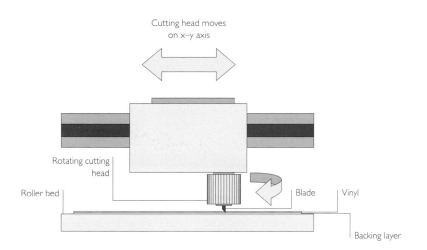

Cutting head moves
on x–y axis

Rotating cutting
head

Roller bed

Blade

Vinyl

Backing layer

Essential Information

VISUAL QUALITY	●●●●●○○○
SPEED	●●●●○○○○
SET-UP COST	●●●●○○○○
UNIT COST	●●●○○○○○
ENVIRONMENT	●●●●○○○○

Related processes include:
- Vinyl Cutting Masking

Alternative and competing processes include:
- Laser Cutting
- Screen Printing

What is Vinyl Cutting?

A vinyl cutter is an x–y plotter, driven by CAD data, except that a sharp blade is used instead of a pen. The cutting head tracks horizontally and the vinyl is moved forwards and backwards on a roller.

Vinyl is polyvinyl chloride (PVC), which for this application is supplied in thicknesses ranging from 0.08–0.8 mm (0.003–0.031 in.) and either matt or gloss.

It is mounted onto a backing layer: the knife cuts through the vinyl, but leaves the backing layer intact.

Intricate and multi-coloured designs can be printed onto white or clear vinyl, as opposed to profiling and registering many individual colour films.

Notes for Designers

QUALITY Vinyl cutting is reasonably precise and vinyl films are long lasting, available in vibrant colours and a range of finishes. It is possible to specify the type of film according to the application, such as indoor, outdoors or backlit.

TYPICAL APPLICATIONS Applications include signs for shops, museums and galleries, banners, wall stickers, exhibition graphics and vehicle graphics.

COST AND SPEED There are no tooling costs. Cycle time is rapid, but weeding can take some time depending on the complexity of the design. Labour costs depend on the extent of the weeding. It is very cost effective for large graphics.

MATERIALS PVC.

ENVIRONMENTAL IMPACTS The waste that is produced by vinyl cutting can be recycled. The downside is that PVC contains chlorine and dioxins. This has led to many campaigns against its use, especially in food, medical and toy applications.

Coloured vinyl Vinyl is available in a wide range of colours, sizes and finishes. The UV stability, durability and light transmission (for backlighting) of the film are selected according to the application.

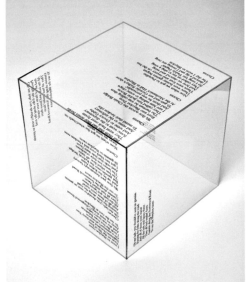

Vinyl on perspex Created by Hawaii Design for the *Our Friends in the North* exhibition, this acrylic box has been decorated with vinyl graphics. The graphics depict verses from the Blaydon Races, a famous song in Newcastle upon Tyne, England.

Featured company Albemarle Graphics Limited
www.ag-online.co.uk

The sharp blade rapidly cuts through the layer of vinyl (image **1**); the speed of the plotter is adjusted according to the intricacy of the design. The parts of the design that are cut out have to be removed by hand. This is known as weeding and is a painstaking task (image **2**).

Afterwards, application tape is applied to the face of the vinyl. The backing layer used to cut the vinyl is removed to reveal the sticky reverse side. The vinyl is then stuck down in its final location, which could be on a wall, a window or a banner. It is rubbed down using a burnisher and the application tape is carefully removed, leaving the vinyl design in place (image **3**).

Cut vinyl is suitable for all scales of application, from small exhibition pieces to large signs, such as these graphics for Tate Modern, London (image **4**).

1

2

3

4

Letterpress

Equally suited to artistic applications and mass production, letterpress is a versatile relief printing process. It is used to print a range of materials, such as for packaging labels, posters and stationery. The printed and embossed surface has a distinctive crafted appearance. It is best suited to printing one or two flat colours.

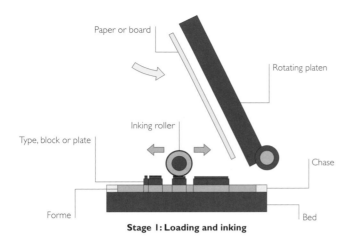

Paper or board

Rotating platen

Inking roller

Type, block or plate

Chase

Forme

Bed

Stage 1: Loading and inking

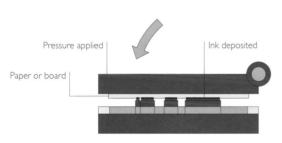

Pressure applied

Ink deposited

Paper or board

Stage 2: Printing

Essential Information

VISUAL QUALITY	●●●●●●○
SPEED	●●●●○○○
SET-UP COST	●●●●○○○
UNIT COST	●●●●●○○
ENVIRONMENT	●●●○○○○

Alternative and competing processes include:

• Embossing and Debossing
• Foil Blocking
• Screen Printing

What is Letterpress?

This is a relief printing process. Ink is applied to the surface of the reversed, raised type. The type is pressed onto the paper to reproduce the positive image, known as right reading.

Traditionally, the type and blocks (for printing images) were carved from wood (see opposite) and assembled into the forme by hand. Individual metal text blocks are used in the same way. This is known as movable type and is measured in points (72 points is 25.4 mm or 1 in.), picas or lines. Modern photo-etched (page 92)

metal plates are more precise and convenient because the individual letters do not need to be assembled for each job. They are manufactured directly from CAD data and usually take no more than a day or two.

Mass-production letterpress is similar to flexography (page 130), except that there is no anilox roll. High volumes are printed with the text wrapped around large rolls.

QUALITY Letterpress is best suited to solid colour printing type, lines and solid blocks of colour. The highest quality of reproduction can be achieved using one or two colours. The texture of the printed material is often visible through the ink.

TYPICAL APPLICATIONS Most applications are relatively low volume and include books, posters, stationery, packaging labels, flyers and invitations.

COST AND SPEED Tooling costs are low, especially if the text blocks are reused, but this is now rare. Cycle time is moderate. Labour costs are high due to the level of craftsmanship required.

MATERIALS This technique is most commonly used to print on paper and board.

ENVIRONMENTAL IMPACTS Utilizing recycled materials reduces the consumption of raw materials. Solvents are required for thinning and cleaning certain inks.

Printing plate and impression (left) This photo-etched (page 92) metal printing plate is the mirror image of the final print. Similar to foil blocking (page 186), the surface of thick and relatively soft materials can be embossed during printing. This creates a distinctive and high quality appearance.

Solid colour poster (above) Low-volume techniques will create printed impressions with varying quality and consistency. This quality is sometimes mimicked in high-volume processes, such as offset lithography (page 124), by digitizing a letterpress sample and reproducing it exactly.

1

Case Study

Letterpress Printing a Block Image

Featured company Modern Activity
www.modernactivity.com

Letterpress printing at Modern Activity is on a Heidelberg, which is suitable for full-scale production. A small measure of ink, which has the consistency of paste, is applied to the rollers (image **1**). As they rotate against one another the ink is evenly distributed.

A pair of rollers pick up a layer of the magenta ink and apply it to the relief parts of the metal printing plate as they travel across the surface (image **2**). Simultaneously, a sheet of paper is loaded onto the platen. The platen rotates and presses the paper onto the inked plate (image **3**).

If the ink is manually rolled onto the plate, then many effects can be achieved, such as the mixing of colours.

The printed pages are removed and checked (image **4**). The quality of reproduction is determined by the plate, ink, paper and distribution of pressure across the surface (image **5**).

2

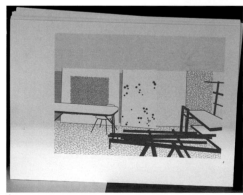

3

4

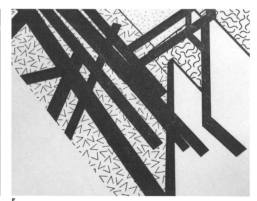

5

Screen Printing

Also known as silkscreen printing, this versatile process is used to apply graphics and coatings onto a range of materials, including paper, glass and plastic. It is employed to print flat and cylindrical parts for diverse applications such as packaging, artwork, stationery and exhibition graphics.

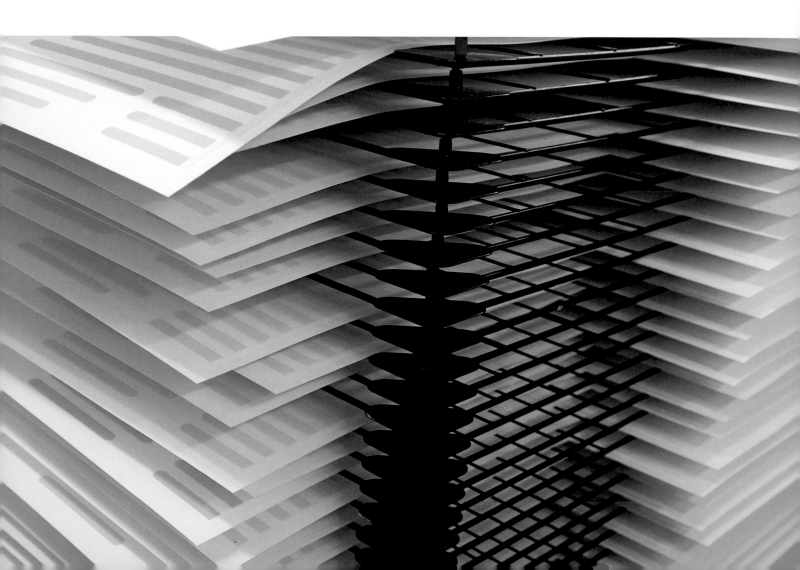

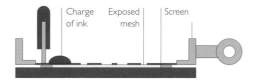

Charge | Exposed | Screen
of ink | mesh |

Stage 1: Load

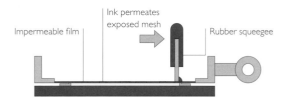

Impermeable film | Ink permeates exposed mesh | Rubber squeegee

Stage 2: Screen print

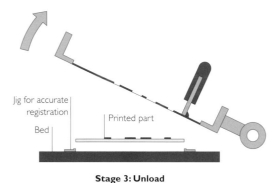

Jig for accurate registration

Bed

Printed part

Stage 3: Unload

Essential Information

VISUAL QUALITY	●●●●●●○
SPEED	●●●●○○○
SET-UP COST	●●○●○●○
UNIT COST	●●●●○○○
ENVIRONMENT	●●●○○○○

Related processes include:
• Discharge Printing
• Screen-making
• Screen Printing Textiles

Alternative and competing processes include:
• Digital Printing
• Foil Blocking
• Pad Printing
• Transfer Printing
• Vinyl Cutting

What is Screen Printing?

This is a wet printing process. A charge of ink is deposited onto the screen and a rubber squeegee is used to spread the ink evenly across the screen. Those areas protected by the impermeable film (stencil) are not printed. The screens are made up of a frame, over which a light mesh is stretched (page 122).

There are four main types of ink: water-based, solvent-based, polyvinyl chloride- (PVC-) based plastisol and ultraviolet (UV) curing. Water and solvent-based inks are air-dried or heated to accelerate the process. PVC-based plastisol inks are used mainly to print textiles. They have varying levels of flexibility, determined by the quantity of plastisol. UV inks contain chemical initiators, which cause polymerization when exposed to UV light. These inks have superior colour and clarity, but are also the most expensive.

QUALITY Screen printing produces graphics with clean edges. The definition of detail and thickness of printed ink is determined by the size of mesh used in the screen. Heavier gauges will deposit more ink, but have lower resolution of detail.

TYPICAL APPLICATIONS Applications are widespread. On packaging, ink can be screen printed directly onto a product's surface, or onto an adhesive label that is bonded to the surface. Screen printing is used to reproduce artwork, exhibition graphics and stationery. Textile applications include bags, clothes and fabrics for interiors. It is also used to apply spot varnish (page 190) and adhesive for gold leaf or flocking (page 176).

COST AND SPEED Tooling costs are low, but depend on the number of colours. Single colour is the least expensive. Mechanized production methods are the most rapid and can print up to 30 parts per minute. The labour costs are moderate to high for manual techniques.

MATERIALS Almost any material can be screen printed, including paper, plastic, rubber, metal, ceramic and glass. There are numerous types of ink such as clear varnish, metallic, pearlescent and fluorescent.

ENVIRONMENTAL IMPACTS PVC-, formaldehyde (UF)- and solvent-based inks contain harmful chemicals, but they can be reclaimed and recycled to avoid water contamination. Screens are recycled (page 122) by dissolving the impermeable film away from the mesh so that it can be reused.

Card packaging (left) Screen printing is used to print high quality text, logos and images directly onto packaging, such as die-cut cartons (page 82), and plastic and glass bottles for cosmetics, food and beverages. The Cork Bird House packaging was designed by Gavin Coyle.

Plastic packaging (above) It is possible to screen print onto almost any type of material depending on the ink technology. This nylon polyester laminated DVD packaging, for Entr'acte, is screen printed and vacuum packed.

1

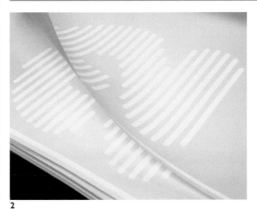

2

3

4

This promotional poster (image **1**) designed by K2 Screen combines several printing and finishing processes. First, the '2' is offset lithography printed (page 124) in luminous yellow (image **2**). The 'K' and '11' are screen printed and the '0' is blind embossed (page 180).

The pre-printed page is loaded onto the screen-printing bed and accurately registered. Ink is applied to the surface of the screen using a spatula (image **3**). A rubber squeegee is used to spread the ink across the surface of the screen (image **4**). Pressure is applied during spreading, to ensure that the ink penetrates the permeable areas of mesh to build up a dense layer of colour with clean edges.

The screen-printed pages are dried in racks (image **5**) before the next printing process begins.

5

Case Study

Printing a Tote Bag

Featured company K2 Screen www.k2screen.co.uk

This cotton bag, designed by MadeThought, has been dyed black and is screen printed with white text (image **1**). Screen printing produces high quality print on textiles, although it is typically more expensive than digital printing (page 138) and transfer printing (page 148), especially when more than one or two colours are required.

The black bag is loaded onto the carousel screen-printing bed (image **2**). It is smoothed flat and held in place by a low-tack adhesive. The screen is lowered down in line with the bag and a layer of ink is screened onto the surface (image **3**). The plastisol ink is sufficiently opaque to cover the black completely (image **4**). Even on textured cloth such as this print quality is very good (image **5**).

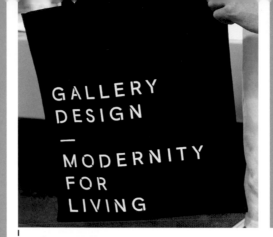

1

2

3

4

5

1

2

3

4

5

Discharge Printing a T-shirt

Featured company K2 Screen www.k2screen.co.uk

Also known as extract printing or colour-discharge printing, discharge printing is an excellent way to produce light coloured prints on dark coloured natural textiles (image **1**). Screen printing is used to apply water-based discharge ink (images **2–4**). The ink undergoes a chemical reaction and removes certain dyes used to colour textiles. This produces light coloured prints with a softer feel than conventional light coloured inks; it is known as 'soft hand'.

The discharge ink is activated by heat (image **5**). Discharge inks can be used alone to simply remove the dye and leave behind the natural colour of the textile, or they can be combined with a dye that is impervious to the discharging agent to add colour to the area that has been discharged.

As a result of removing dye it may not always be possible to match colours, such as Pantone or RAL, or produce bright whites and other challenging colours.

Discharge printing is utilized for gaming tables because, unlike with conventional inks, there is not an edge to the print. It is also used for large areas of print because it does not affect the handle of the textile like plastisol ink.

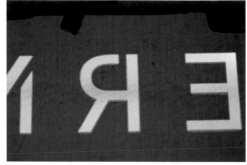

Reusing screens Screens can be used to reproduce several thousand prints, or they can be reused many times for shorter print runs. The ink and stencil are dissolved and washed away to leave the bare mesh, which can be recoated with emulsion and a new stencil created.

Mesh and emulsion The density of the mesh determines the quantity of ink deposited onto the surface. Very fine details reproduce precisely with the photographic process. It is possible to reproduce details down to 0.3 mm (0.012 in. or 1 pt.). With UV curing inks, and depending on the surface area, even finer details measuring 0.15 mm (0.005 in. or 0.5 pt.) can be reproduced.

Case Study

Preparing a Screen

Featured company K2 Screen www.k2screen.co.uk

This case study demonstrates the process of preparing a screen for printing the K2 poster (page 119).

The screens are made up of a frame, over which a light mesh is stretched. The mesh is typically made up of nylon, polyester or stainless steel. The type and density of mesh is selected according to the ink, design and level of detail sought. Each colour requires a separate screen.

First of all, the screen is carefully cleaned and coated with emulsion (image **1**). Once the emulsion is dry the screen is loaded onto a vacuum table along with the negative (image **2**). The design is printed in black onto transparent acetate. A separate negative is produced for each colour and screen. It works by blocking the selected parts of the screen from exposure to UV light (image **3**).

Areas of the emulsion exposed to UV light harden. Unexposed areas are washed away with water (image **4**). This creates the durable and precise stencil screen ready for printing.

1

2

3

4

Offset Lithography

The most common commercial printing technique for magazines, catalogues and books, including this one, offset lithography is a very rapid and low cost method of reproducing high quality images and text. A print is created as a result of the basic principle that oil and water do not mix.

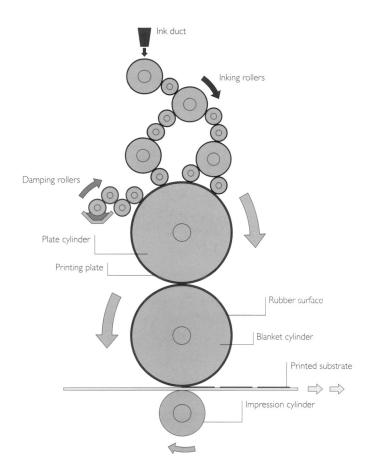

Ink duct

Inking rollers

Damping rollers

Plate cylinder

Printing plate

Rubber surface

Blanket cylinder

Printed substrate

Impression cylinder

Essential Information

VISUAL QUALITY	●●●●●●● ○
SPEED	●●●●●● ○ ○
SET-UP COST	●●●●●● ○ ○
UNIT COST	●●● ○ ○ ○ ○ ○
ENVIRONMENT	●●●● ○ ○ ○ ○

Related processes include:
• Sheet-fed
• Tinplate Printing
• Web-fed

Alternative and competing processes include:
• Digital Printing
• Flexography
• Rotogravure

What is Offset Lithography?

Often simply referred to as offset litho, this process relies on the basic principle that oil and water do not mix. The non-image areas on the printing plate absorb water, whereas the image areas repel water (hydrophobic). During printing, the damping rollers keep the plate wet. The ink, which is oily, is fed from the ink duct onto the ink rollers (known collectively as the ink pyramid) and distributed evenly. The ink is repelled by the wet areas and sticks to the image areas that remain dry.

The ink is transferred to the rubber surface on the blanket cylinder, which is pressed against the paper as it rotates, creating a sharp and well-defined print. This indirect method of printing is known as 'offset'. It is most commonly associated with mass-production lithographic printing, but is also utilized for other printing techniques.

QUALITY The flexible rubber on the blanket cylinder conforms to the printed surface, ensuring a high quality image with sharp edges. The individual dots of ink grow throughout the printing process. This is known as dot gain and is greater on more absorbent substrates.

TYPICAL APPLICATIONS Typical applications include packaging, books (this one, for example), magazines, newspapers and similar products. Other large-scale applications include banknotes (in combination with rotogravure and letterpress) and printing directly onto tinplate for packaging and toys.

COST AND SPEED Tooling costs are high, making this process less practical for short production runs. Cycle time is very rapid and web presses can print hundreds of metres per minute. A perfecting press prints both sides in a single pass. Labour costs are moderate due to the skills required.

MATERIALS Sheet materials, including paper, card, board and metal.

ENVIRONMENTAL IMPACTS The choice of ink, substrate and finishing (such as varnishing) affect the environmental impact of offset lithography. UV-cured inks are low in solvent or contain no solvents at all. Utilizing recycled materials reduces the consumption of raw materials; solvents are required for thinning and cleaning certain inks.

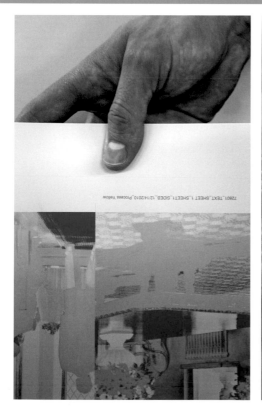

Offset lithography printing plate A plate like this is required for each colour. First of all, the image and text are separated into individual colours, including the process colours (CMYK) and spot colours if required. In operation, water sticks to non-image areas and ink to the areas that are not wet.

The plate is produced directly from computer data in a process known as computer to plate (CTP). This is a recent development that has revolutionized plate-making by eliminating a stage in the process, improving quality and reducing turnaround time.

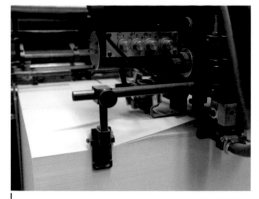

1

2

3

4

5

Case Study

Printing a Catalogue

Featured company Colchester Print Group
www.brecklandprint.com

There are two main techniques: sheet-fed and web-fed. Sheet-fed uses a stack of sheets of paper, such as in this case (image **1**), which are individually loaded, whereas web-fed uses a large roll of paper and is utilized for higher volumes.

Ink is deposited onto the inking roller (image **2**). A separate printing plate (see opposite) is required for each of the process colours. Used in combination, CMYK (image **3**) creates full-colour images. Special colours, such as spot colours for company logos, require a separate print plate and an additional colour station.

The pages are stacked (image **4**) ready for binding (page 194). Anti-set-off powder is applied to the surface of each sheet to separate them and stop ink rub-off.

The quality and consistency are measured by a densitometer using colour calibration bars (image **5**). Each of the keys controls the quantity of ink applied to that part of the ink roller and thus the printing plate.

Direct printing onto metal Instead of printing onto a white basecoat, which increases cost, it is possible to print onto a clear pre-coating, known as size, to maintain the metallic colour.

Offset lithography printing onto metal is precise and fine details reproduce well. However, unlike paper, metal does not absorb any ink whatsoever. This can affect the size of details, such as type, that can be reproduced within a printed background.

Harrods biscuit tin A typical application for printed tinplate is specialty packaging, such as this biscuit tin for Harrods, London. It is embossed (page 180), press formed (page 42) and joined along the seam (page 48). Other packaging applications include aerosols, oil drums, lever lid tins, cosmetic products and food containers.

Case Study

Offset Lithography Printing Tinplate

Featured company Cyril Luff Metal Decorators Ltd
www.cyrilluff.co.uk

Sheet metals, including aluminium, steel and tinplate, are printed before being formed into packaging containers.

Tinplate (image **1**) is steel electroplated with a thin layer of tin to prevent corrosion. In preparation, the sheets are cut to size, pre-coated with a white basecoat and dried in an oven (image **2**). The white basecoat ensures that colours look clean and vibrant. It is also possible to maintain the metallic colour (above, left).

Offset lithography printing sheet metal is just the same as printing onto paper (page 127) (image **3**). The inks are UV

1

2

cured (image **4**), which is rapid and means that there are fewer solvents, or none at all.

The printed and varnished sheets are stacked (image **5**) ready for shipping to a factory where they will be formed into containers. The difference in colour between printing on white and clear is visible in the finished part (image **6**).

3

4

5

6

Flexography

Also known as flexo, this relief printing technique is used to reproduce images and text onto a range of materials. Continuous improvements in the presses, plate-making and ink technology have increased demand for flexography in many applications, including packaging labels, bags, cartons and colour newspapers.

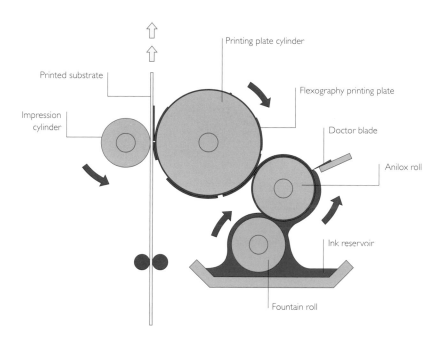

Printing plate cylinder

Printed substrate

Flexography printing plate

Impression cylinder

Doctor blade

Anilox roll

Ink reservoir

Fountain roll

Essential Information

VISUAL QUALITY	●●●●●●○
SPEED	●●●●●○○
SET-UP COST	●●●○○○○
UNIT COST	●●○○○○○
ENVIRONMENT	●●●○○○○

Alternative and competing processes include:
- Digital Printing
- Offset Lithography
- Rotogravure

What is Flexography?

Flexography is similar to letterpress in that the ink is transferred from a relief printing plate onto the substrate.

This process operates at high speed. The ink is picked up by a fountain roll from the reservoir and transferred to the anilox roll, which has a hard ceramic coating. The surface is covered completely with minute cells, which collect a precise measure of ink controlled by the doctor blade. The anilox roll presses against the plate, which is mounted on the plate cylinder. The counter rotation of the cylinders is synchronized.

The relief parts of the plate pick up the layer of ink from the anilox roll and, in turn, transfer it to the substrate, which is fed between the rotating plate and impression cylinder.

Notes for Designers

QUALITY Modern flexography printing technology rivals offset lithography (page 124) in some cases, such as for full colour newspapers, as a result of improved quality, reduced cost and improved flexibility (in terms of inks and materials).

TYPICAL APPLICATIONS It is used for diverse applications, including packaging labels, plastic bags (see blown film extrusion, page 60), cardboard boxes (page 81), cartons, magazines, newspapers and wallpaper.

COST AND SPEED Tooling costs are low and have been improved by recent photopolymer plate developments (see below, left). This means that for low volumes, flexography is less expensive than offset lithography (page 124). Cycle time is very rapid: a rate of 100 m (330 ft.) per minute or more is possible. Labour costs are moderate because a high level of skill and experience is required.

MATERIALS Sheets and rolls of paper, card, plastic, corrugate, glass, metal, metalized films and textile can all be printed in this way.

ENVIRONMENTAL IMPACTS Utilizing recycled materials reduces the consumption of raw materials. Solvents are required for thinning and cleaning certain inks. UV curing systems require the least ink and energy.

Flexography printing plate Photopolymer plates are made by exposing a sheet of photosensitive plastic to UV light behind a printed negative. Unexposed areas remain soft and are washed away to create the relief printing plate, which is mounted directly onto the plate cylinder (page 131).

Printed foil wrapping Aluminium foil wrapping, such as for these handmade Max Perry chocolates, are printed by flexography. Inks printed over the top have a metalized look because the silver is visible through the layers.

1

2

Case Study

Flexography Printing Adhesive Labels

Featured company Colchester Print Group
www.brecklandprint.com

The self-adhesive labels for Hillfarm rapeseed oil (image **1**) are flexography printed on a five-colour press using the four process colours (CMYK) and a gold spot colour. A roll of self-adhesive label with backing paper is fed into the print line where it is printed, coated and cut out in a continuous process known as in-line (image **2**).

First of all, key (black) is printed (image **3**) followed by yellow (image **4**), magenta and then cyan. In this case, gold is added as a spot colour to highlight a design detail. The inks are cured with exposure to UV light: between each colour station the printed labels pass under a UV light (image **5**). This greatly accelerates the process.

Finally, the labels are kiss cut (see die cutting, page 76), trimmed and wound onto a take-up spool (image **6**).

3

4

5

6

Rotogravure

Also known as gravure, this is an intaglio printing process capable of producing continuous tone images. The print cylinders are expensive, so rotogravure is typically reserved for print runs of 250,000 or more. Modern presses are capable of printing 14 m (46 ft.) of paper per second.

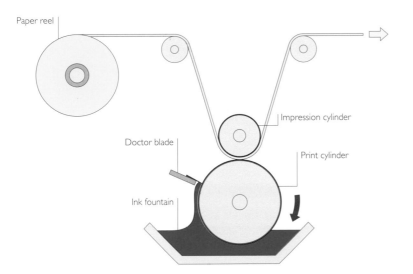

Paper reel

Doctor blade

Ink fountain

Impression cylinder

Print cylinder

VISUAL QUALITY	●●●●●●○○
SPEED	●●●●●●●○
SET-UP COST	●●●●●●●○
UNIT COST	●○○○○○●○
ENVIRONMENT	●●●●○○○○

Alternative and competing processes include:
- Flexography
- Offset Lithography

What is Rotogravure?

This is an intaglio process, which means the ink is transferred from recesses, known as cells, in the print cylinder onto the paper or other material. The steel cylinder is copper plated. The cells are formed by engraving with a diamond-tipped stylus, or a laser, and the finished cylinder is chrome plated for durability.

A cylinder is required for each colour. It is partially submerged in the ink fountain, coating the surface. Solvent-based inks provide the fastest cycle time because they can be dried more quickly than water-based inks.

A doctor blade wipes the excess ink from the surface of the cylinder (on the non-printed areas). Ink left in the cells is transferred to the paper as it passes between the print cylinder and rubber-coated impression cylinder.

Rotogravure is a high-volume and rapid process and so is typically used to print onto reels of paper. This is known as web-fed.

Notes for Designers

QUALITY Rotogravure is the only high speed, high volume print process capable of producing continuous tone images. Reproduction is not as sharp as offset lithography (page 124) and flexography (page 130) because the ink dots blend together: this is most noticeable in small type.

TYPICAL APPLICATIONS Used to print large volumes of magazines, newspaper inserts, wallpaper, packaging, wrapping paper and greeting cards.

COST AND SPEED Tooling costs are high. Cycle time is very rapid: modern presses are capable of printing 14m (46 ft.) of paper per second. Labour costs are low because the process is largely automated.

MATERIALS Predominantly used to print rolls of paper, it is also used for plastic packaging, such as polypropylene (PP), polyethylene (PE) and polyethylene terephthalate (PET).

ENVIRONMENTAL IMPACTS Rotogravure mainly uses solvent-based ink due to its rapid drying time. Solvent evaporates into the atmosphere and so has to be absorbed and contained by an extraction system.

Case Study

Printing a Glossy Magazine

Featured company Polestar
www.polestar-group.com

Steel cylinders, machined to precise dimensions, are plated with copper. Cells are engraved into the copper layer with diamond-tipped styluses (image **1**). The print cylinder is then plated with chrome to create a very hard and durable outer layer (image **2**). This is essential for ensuring the highest quality on large print runs.

The depth and width of the cells on the print cylinder are varied to adjust the quantity of ink applied to the paper. Deeper cells will hold more ink and so produce a darker colour dot, whereas shallow cells hold less ink. The dots of ink partially blend together to form continuous tone colour.

A roll, or web, of paper is loaded onto the print press (image **3**). In this case, each roll weighs 3,326 kg (7,332 lbs.). The paper is fed into the printer and pressed against each of the print cylinders (image **4**).

The process operates at very high speed: several million printed pages are produced each hour. To manage the huge output, the sheets are split into strips, cut and folded into folios and then the output is taken up on large rolls (image **5**).

When all the pages have been printed they are gathered together (image **6**) and saddle stitched (page 72). The finishing magazine is welded (page 64) into a plastic sleeve ready for shipping (image **7**).

1

2

3

4

5

6

7

Digital Printing

In these processes, digital files are outputted directly to the printer. It is inexpensive for low volumes because print plates are not required and there is little or no set-up cost. The quality and speed varies according to whether it is laser or ink jet printing.

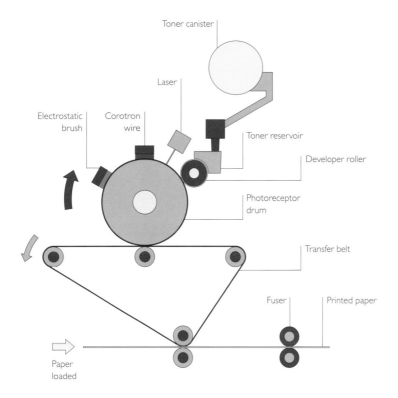

Toner canister

Laser

Electrostatic brush

Corotron wire

Toner reservoir

Developer roller

Photoreceptor drum

Transfer belt

Fuser

Printed paper

Paper loaded

Essential Information

VISUAL QUALITY	● ● ● ● ● ● ● ●
SPEED	● ● ● ● ● ○ ○ ○
SET-UP COST	○ ● ● ● ● ● ● ●
UNIT COST	● ● ● ● ● ● ○ ○
ENVIRONMENT	● ● ● ○ ○ ○ ○ ○

Related processes include:

• Ink jet
• Laser

Alternative and competing processes include:

• Flexography
• Letterpress
• Offset Lithography
• Risography
• Screen Printing

What is Laser Printing?

Laser printing uses laser-guided electrostatic energy to transfer toner powder onto paper in the form of text and images. As the photoreceptor drum rotates it is cleaned and discharged by an electrostatic brush. The corotron wire then applies a positive electrostatic charge to the entire surface. A laser 'writes' text and images onto the surface by discharging areas. The fine toner power, which is positively charged, sticks to these areas.

The toner is deposited onto the transfer belt, which is travelling at speed, and then transferred from the belt onto the surface of the pages as they pass beneath and

are pressed onto it. For colour printing, all four colours are applied to the belt to create the complete image to be transferred to the paper, whereas in monochrome printing the toner is applied directly to the paper.

As the paper moves through the printer, the toner is heated and pressed onto the paper by a pair of heated rolls, known as the fuser. This 'fixes' it permanently by melting the plastic onto the surface of the paper (page 140). Alternative curing systems include UV and air-drying.

Notes for Designers

QUALITY Ink jet printing, also known under trade names such as Giclée, produces superb quality prints. The quality and consistency of laser printing is not particularly high, but is steadily improving.

TYPICAL APPLICATIONS On flexible substrates, such as books, labels, brochures and stationery, digital printing competes with offset lithography (page 124) and flexography (page 130). For rigid substrates used for point-of-sale and table tops, for example, it competes with screen printing (page 116).

COST AND SPEED Digital printing is very cost effective for up to 1,000 prints because no plates are required. Cycle time is rapid: laser printers can reproduce 100 pages per minute, whereas ink jet is slower. Labour costs are low.

MATERIALS Includes paper, plastic and textile; and rigid substrates such as board, wood and glass. The type of printing will determine the type of material used.

ENVIRONMENTAL IMPACTS These are low impact processes because a precise amount of ink is deposited and there is very little waste. Recycled materials and bio-based inks further reduce environmental impact.

Laser printed finish The toner used in laser printing is made up of pigment and plastic. The fusing process, whereby the toner is melted and pressed onto the substrate, creates a glossy finish.

Registration is precise in laser printing, even at very high speeds. Both images and text have good edge definition.

Case Study

Colour Press Proofing

Featured company Colchester Print Group
www.brecklandprint.com

Unlike conventional printing processes,
such as offset lithography (page 124)
and flexography (page 130), the image
is transferred directly to the print press.
In other words, no plates or screens
are required.

An operator makes adjustments to the
colour output levels in Adobe Acrobat
(image **1**), which is used to transfer the
digital file to the print press as PostScript.

These systems use a dedicated
four colour process (image **2**), so it
is not possible to use spot colours.
This also means it is not possible to match
all colours: for instance, specific Pantone
references cannot be matched.

The full colour print emerges within
seconds and is checked by the printer
against the colour target (image **3**).
Continuous tone images, such as
photographs, can be reproduced
very well using laser printing (image **4**).
Despite this, offset lithography and
flexography are considered superior.

1

2

3

4

What is Ink Jet Printing?

Similar to laser printing, ink jet printing does not require print plates: the data is transferred directly from a computer to the printer using RIP software.

Ink is squeezed through tiny orifices around 10 microns (0.0004 in.) in diameter directly onto the paper, which is 1 mm (0.04 in.) below. However, certain printers, known as direct to material (DTM), are capable of printing onto textured and uneven surfaces, including wood and textile.

Pressure is applied to the ink by either thermal or piezoelectric means. In thermal ink jet printing, the heater causes the ink in contact with it to expand rapidly, forcing the ink in the orifice onto the paper. It cools and the cycle is repeated many times per second.

Piezoelectric materials deform when an electrical field is applied. This forces the diaphragm downward and subsequently an ink droplet is discharged from the orifice.

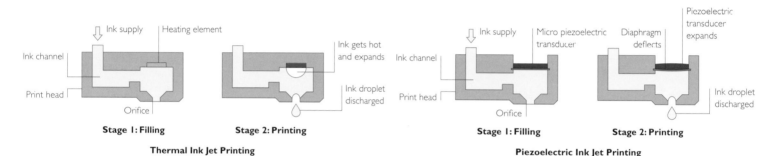

Thermal Ink Jet Printing

Stage 1: Filling — Stage 2: Printing

Ink supply | Heating element | Ink channel | Print head | Orifice | Ink gets hot and expands | Ink droplet discharged

Piezoelectric Ink Jet Printing

Stage 1: Filling — Stage 2: Printing

Ink supply | Micro piezoelectric transducer | Diaphragm deflects | Piezoelectric transducer expands | Ink channel | Print head | Orifice | Ink droplet discharged

Print resolution Layers of dots of translucent ink are built up gradually to achieve very high quality prints. It is not uncommon for each swath of the image to take six or more passes of the print head. Resolution is typically between 600–1200 dots per inch (DPI) and is determined by the requirements of the application.

Ink Jet Printing a Poster

Featured company Albemarle Graphics Limited
www.ag-online.co.uk

The poster design is checked before printing (image **1**). Paper is loaded into the printer and the process begins. The image is built up in swathes: a complete pass of the printer head from right to left (image **2**). Printing is rapid, even though each swath requires six passes of the print head to achieve 720 dots per inch (DPI). Like conventional printing processes, such as offset lithography (page 124), ink jet printing is based on the CMYK process colour system (image **3**). In addition to the basic colours, it is possible to add lighter shades of cyan, magenta, yellow and ketone (grey) to ensure the highest quality light tones in photographic images and graphic designs. The printed poster is laminated with a clear protective plastic cover and rigid foam board base (image **4**). Finally, it is trimmed to size (image **5**).

Risography

This is a high speed and low cost process. Risography has a low environmental impact and the print quality has a distinctive, grainy appearance. It is used to print from a digital file or to reproduce a scanned original. The ink drums are interchangeable so it can be used to apply any number of colours individually or registered.

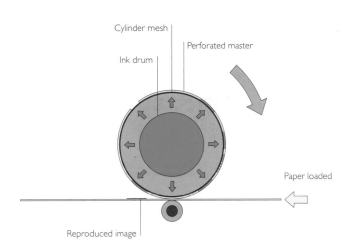

Cylinder mesh

Perforated master

Ink drum

Paper loaded

Reproduced image

Essential Information

VISUAL QUALITY	●●○○○○○○
SPEED	●●●●●●○○
SET-UP COST	●○○○○○○○
UNIT COST	●●○○○○○○
ENVIRONMENT	●●○○○○○○

Alternative and competing processes include:
- Digital Printing
- Flexography
- Letterpress
- Offset Lithography

What is Risography?

Risography is a digital and high speed stencil printing process. It is like screen printing (page 116), but the reproduction quality is very different. First of all, the master is created, either from digital data or by scanning an existing artwork. Tiny holes, which correspond to the areas of colour, are burnt into the master sheet by laser. Each colour requires its own master.

The master sheet is wrapped around the ink drum. Ink is pressed through the cylinder screen, but masked by the master as the ink drum rotates at high speed. The paper passes underneath, registered to the location of the master, and ink is applied to the surface. Modern presses can reproduce over 120 pages per minute.

Presses are either one or two colour. So, the ink drum is changed for each colour, or pair of colours, and the paper is reloaded and reprinted.

QUALITY Risography has a very distinctive quality, which can be used to artistic advantage. Registration is not precise.

TYPICAL APPLICATIONS Typically used to reproduce flyers, such as for schools and political parties, posters, stationery, forms and invitations.

COST AND SPEED For volumes of 50 or more risography is usually less expensive than digital printing (page 138) and photocopying. For several thousand prints or more offset lithography (page 124) and flexography (page 130) will be less expensive. Tooling costs are minimal, but colour ink drums are expensive. Cycle time is very rapid. Labour costs are low.

MATERIALS Paper.

ENVIRONMENTAL IMPACTS The environmental impacts for this process are relatively low. Since 2001, soy-based ink has been available for use in risography. Soybean oil is less expensive and less energy intensive to produce than petroleum-derived inks and it contains less volatile organic compounds (VOC), which cause air pollution. A small amount of ink is needed because soybean oil produces rich and bright colours. Unlike with laser printers, the ink does not need to be fixed with heat. They are easily removed in the de-inking process used in recycling and using recycled paper further reduces the environmental impact.

Registration Large areas of solid colour will show the most variation. The quality of registration is not as good as laser printing (page 139) because each colour is applied separately. It uses interchangeable ink drums, so different colours and spot colours can be used.

   The inks used are similar to offset lithography (page 124), so can be printed over with laser printing to create individual items, such as serial numbers.

Case Study

Risograph Printing a Booking Form

Featured company Modern Activity
www.modernactivity.com

In the past, and because it is very low cost, risography was utilized mainly by schools, political parties and churches to duplicate flyers and pamphlets, for example. Now artists and designers use it, because of its distinctive visual quality, to print, for example, invitations, books, flyers and artwork.

The risography print press looks similar to a photocopier (image **1**) and has the same size footprint. The master is created and placed onto the ink drum (image **2**). The tiny holes are visible on the surface. As the drum rotates at high speed ink is forced through the holes by centrifugal force.

The print quality is distinctive and print marks and blemishes are unavoidable (image **3**).

is your Table Bo
erial Worlds, to
use, Bloomsbury
4DA on 9 Marcl

h this booking form to: Dida Tait, Cont
3QL. T: 020 7831 3217   F: 020 7831 1214

Dye Sublimation Printing

Also known as heat transfer printing, images are reproduced onto flat or 3D surfaces by a transfer medium that is wrapped around the form. The types of printed effects that can be achieved are similar to ink jet printing, which is used to create the transfers.

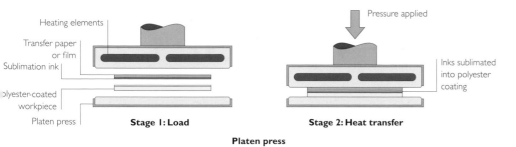

Heating elements

Transfer paper
or film

Sublimation ink

Polyester-coated
workpiece

Platen press

Stage 1: Load

Pressure applied

Inks sublimated
into polyester
coating

Stage 2: Heat transfer

Platen press

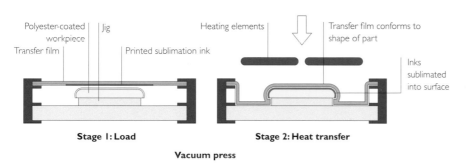

Polyester-coated
workpiece

Jig

Transfer film

Printed sublimation ink

Heating elements

Transfer film conforms to
shape of part

Inks
sublimated
into surface

Stage 1: Load

Stage 2: Heat transfer

Vacuum press

Essential Information

VISUAL QUALITY	●●●●●●○
SPEED	●●●●○○○
SET-UP COST	●●●●●○○
UNIT COST	●●●●●●○
ENVIRONMENT	●●●●○○○

Alternative and competing processes include:

- Decal Printing
- Hydro Transfer Printing
- In-mold Decoration
- Pad Printing
- Screen Printing

What is Dye Sublimation Printing?

The workpiece is coated with a specially developed polyurethane or polyester coating. It is also possible, however, to print directly (without a coating) onto polybutylene terephthalate (PBT) when utilizing IDT Systems' 3D in-surface imaging process (page 151). The transfer film is typically paper or plastic film and is printed with sublimation inks. The image on the transfer medium is reversed because it will be mirrored during the transfer process to be 'right reading' once printed.

Dye sublimation printing is either carried out on a rigid platen or by forming the transfer film to the shape of the part to be printed. Both work on the same principles.

In stage 1, the transfer medium and workpiece are loaded into the press. In stage 2, the press is closed and pressure (or vacuum) is maintained for 2–5 minutes. Heat and pressure cause the inks on the transfer medium to sublimate into the plastic coating. Sublimation means that the inks transfer between the surfaces without melting.

QUALITY The image quality is determined by the print process and print resolution on the transfer medium. Colour intensity is also affected by the colour of material that is being printed.

TYPICAL APPLICATIONS Applications include consumer electronics, sports products (skis, snowboards and helmets) and even bicycle wheels.

COST AND SPEED There are no tooling costs for platen and vacuum techniques. However, there is a cost associated with jigs, the production of the transfer and computer software for digital printing. Cycle time is good and labour costs are low.

MATERIALS Wood, metal, glass and ceramic can all be printed if they are coated. Due to the requirement for heat and pressure to be applied this limits the range of plastics that can be printed to PBT, polycarbonate (PC), PC/PBT, polyethylene terephthalate (PET), polyoxymethylene (POM) and polyamide (PA).

ENVIRONMENTAL IMPACTS The coating is applied by spray painting, which is usually carried out in a booth or cabinet to allow the paints to be recycled and disposed of safely. Water-based paints are less toxic than solvent-borne. However, with IDT Systems' process it is possible to print directly onto PBT, including recycled grades, without a topcoat, thus reducing the associated environmental impacts. The only other waste produced is the transfer medium, which can usually be recycled.

Camouflaged gun stock Just like hydro transfer printing (page 162), dye sublimation printing is used to decorate undulating 3D surfaces with full colour images. The graphic wraps around the contours with little or no distortion. Unlike hydro transfer printing, there is no need to finish the printed part with a protective topcoat.

Perfume packaging One of the advantages of dye sublimation is that it can be used to decorate almost any material, such as this glass bottle. The option of ink jet printing (page 142) the transfer means that it is utilized in the production of special editions and limited production runs as well as high-volume production of identical parts.

1

2

3

4

3D Dye Sublimation Printing a Phone Cover

Featured company IDT Systems
www.idt-systems.com

This case study demonstrates IDT Systems' 3D in-surface imaging process. As a result of using ink jet printing (page 142), the transfer of each mobile phone cover can be decorated with a unique image. These protective covers for the iPhone 3 are injection molded (page 52) polycarbonate (PC) (image **1**).

The transfer film, which has a metallic coating on the back to protect it from the heat, is clamped into the vacuum frame on top of the parts, with the printed side facing down (images **2** and **3**). The whole assembly is loaded into the vacuum chamber. With the application of heat and pressure the film conforms to the 3D surface profile (image **4**). The ink becomes gaseous and sublimates into the surface coating. Using a vacuum means that small undercuts can be achieved.

After around six minutes from when the images were chosen, the transfer film is removed to reveal the printed surface (image **5**).

5

Decal Printing

Also known as bat printing or transfer printing, this transfer technique is used to produce flush, high quality and durable graphics on glazed ceramics. Several printing processes are used to create the transfers, including ink jet, screen printing and offset lithography. As a result, it is utilized for all volumes of production.

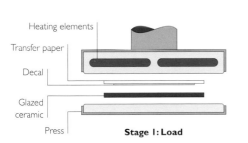

Transfer paper — Decal separates — Water bath

Stage 1: Soak

Decal transferred onto surface — Glazed ceramic

Stage 2: Waterslide transfer

Waterslide transfer

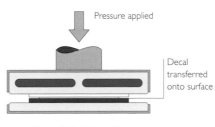

Heating elements
Transfer paper
Decal
Glazed ceramic
Press

Stage 1: Load

Pressure applied

Decal transferred onto surface

Stage 2: Heat transfer

Heat transfer

Essential Information

VISUAL QUALITY	●●●●●●○
SPEED	●●●○○○○
SET-UP COST	●●●○○○○
UNIT COST	●●●●●○○
ENVIRONMENT	●●●●○○○

Related processes include:
• Heat Transfer
• Waterslide Transfer

Alternative and competing processes include:
• Dye Sublimation Printing
• Hydro Transfer Printing
• In-mold Decoration
• Pad Printing
• Screen Printing

What is Decal Printing?

There are two principal techniques for applying the decal: waterslide and heat transfer.

In waterslide, the printed decal is held onto the paper transfer by a water-soluble adhesive. In stage 1, the transfer is soaked in a bath of water to separate the decal. The inks are held together by a delicate varnish topcoat, which is burnt away during firing. In stage 2, the decal is rubbed onto the surface of the workpiece using a cloth or squeegee.

In heat transfer, the printed decal is transferred directly onto the substrate using pressure and heat. In stage 1, the decal and workpiece are loaded into the press. In stage 2, heat and pressure cause the decal to transfer onto the surface of the workpiece.

Finally, the parts are fired. The high temperature reached during firing causes the inks to be drawn into the glaze to create a smooth and durable finish.

QUALITY Similar to dye sublimation printing (page 148), the image quality is determined by the print process and print resolution on the transfer medium. The surface is very durable and will not wear or wash away.

TYPICAL APPLICATIONS Applications include ceramic tableware, bottles, packaging, jewelry, tiles and cookware. Glazed ceramics are also known as glostware.

COST AND SPEED Tooling and set-up costs are determined by the method of printing. Cycle time is slow due to the many stages in transfer printing. Labour costs depend on the complexity of the decoration.

MATERIALS All types of ceramic, including earthenware, stoneware and porcelain.

ENVIRONMENTAL IMPACTS The only waste produced is the transfer medium and that can usually be recycled. The products are durable and long lasting. However, the firing process is energy intensive and therefore the kiln is fully loaded for each firing cycle.

Transfer-printed porcelain Colour images and fine details reproduce very well on the surface of glazed ceramic. The Runo Summer Ray design is screen printed (page 116). For larger volumes offset lithography printing (page 124) can be utilized to reduce cost. Historically, the decal was made using copperplate printing. This technique was developed to provide a cost effective alternative to hand painting enamel decorations and had a significant impact on the manufacture and design of pottery.

1

Waterslide Transfer Printing an Arabia Runo Summer Ray Plate

Featured company Arabia Finland
www.arabia.fi

This case study shows decal printing a Runo plate designed by Heini Riitahuhta (see also pages 158, 160 and 161). There are four designs in the series, which represent the different seasons: spring, summer, autumn and winter. This pattern is Summer Ray (image **1**).

First of all, the plates are glaze-fired. The decal is separated (image **2**) and the ink is transferred onto the glazed piece with the varnish membrane intact (image **3**). The ink and varnish are rubbed onto the surface to remove any excess water and trapped air (image **4**).

A second, high temperature firing cycle at 1,120°C (2,048°F) causes the inks to be permanently drawn into the glaze. This creates a very durable finish.

2

3

4

Pad Printing

Pad printing, also known as tampo printing, is used to print on surfaces that are flat, concave, convex or even both concave and convex. This is possible because the ink is applied to the product using a flexible silicone pad, which wraps around the surface of the part without loss of shape or quality.

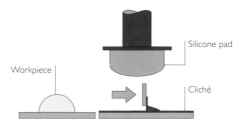

Workpiece

Silicone pad

Cliché

Stage 1: Preparation

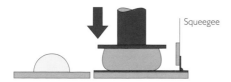

Squeegee

Stage 2: Pick-up

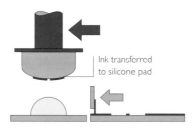

Ink transferred
to silicone pad

Stage 3: Transfer

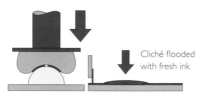

Cliché flooded
with fresh ink

Stage 4: Print

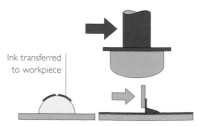

Ink transferred
to workpiece

Stage 5: Finish

Essential Information

VISUAL QUALITY	●●●●●●○○
SPEED	●●●●○○○○
SET-UP COST	●●○○○○○○
UNIT COST	●●●●○○○○
ENVIRONMENT	●●○○○○○○

Related processes include:
• Rotary Pad Printing

Alternative and competing processes include:
• Dye Sublimation Printing
• Hydro Transfer Printing
• Screen Printing

What is Pad Printing?

In stage 1, the cliché is flooded with ink. The engraved design in the cliché is very shallow: the same thickness as the finished print. In stage 2, the silicone pad picks up the ink from the cliché.

In stage 3, the silicone pad moves over to the product. Meanwhile, the squeegee tracks back across the cliché, which is about to be flooded with ink again.

In stage 4, the silicone pad is compressed onto the workpiece. It wraps around the surface profile and the ink is transferred to the surface.

In stage 5, the part is finished and the silicone pad tracks back to the cliché, where a fresh charge of ink has been flooded and wiped clean.

Notes for Designers

QUALITY The definition of detail is determined by the design of the cliché and can incorporate details 0.1 mm (0.004 in.) thick spaced 0.1 mm (0.004 in.) apart. The smooth silicone will transfer all of the ink it picks up onto the surface of the part.

TYPICAL APPLICATIONS As well as ceramic tableware, pad printing is used to decorate keypads in handheld devices, such as remote controls, and it is used to apply logos (page 13), instructions and images onto many items of sports equipment.

COST AND SPEED Tooling costs are low and each pad lasts several thousand cycles. Cycle time is rapid and labour costs are low.

MATERIALS Almost all materials can be printed in this way. Some plastic materials will require surface pre-treatment to ensure high print quality.

ENVIRONMENTAL IMPACTS This process is limited to solvent-based inks and associated thinners that may contain harmful chemicals.

Multiple colour pad printing If multiple colours are required, such as for the Arabia Runo plate, they are separated into individual elements in the process. In other words, each colour requires a separate cliché and silicone pad. Inks can be laid down wet-on-wet, which is an advantage for multiple colour printing.

1

2

3

4

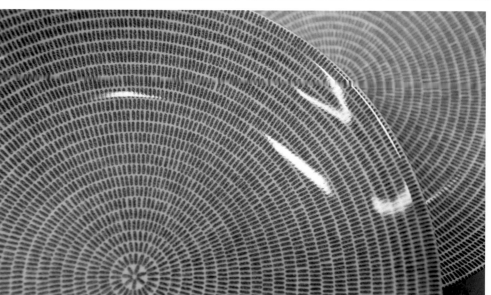

5

Pad Printing the Arabia Avec Plate

Featured company Arabia Finland www.arabia.fi

Stacks of glaze-fired plates are loaded into the automated printing process (image **1**). The design is etched into the cliché and the large silicone pad picks up a layer of ink (image **2**) by pressing onto the cliché.

The silicone pad aligns with the plate, is pushed into it and conforms to the convex shape without distorting the image (image **3**). On contact, the ink is deposited onto the surface of the glaze. The quality of each print is carefully inspected (image **4**). During a second firing cycle the ink is drawn into the glaze and forms a permanent and hard-wearing surface decoration (image **5**).

What is Rotary Pad Printing?

Rotary pad printing is suitable for both flat and cylindrical parts. It is a very rapid process and small items, such as bottle tops, can be printed at speeds up to 120,000 parts per hour.

The cliché is cylindrical and rotated against a doctor blade as it is coated with ink. The blade removes excess ink to ensure a high quality print. Through rotation the ink is transferred to the silicone pad, which in turn rotates against the workpiece. The ink is applied onto the surface of the workpiece as the cliché is flooded with fresh ink ready for the next cycle.

As well as printing individual layers of ink, rotary pad printing is used to transfer pre-printed images directly from decals (see opposite).

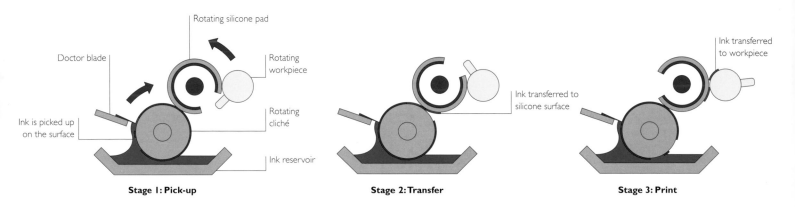

Stage 1: Pick-up   Stage 2: Transfer   Stage 3: Print

Arabia Runo mug collection The Runo mugs, designed by Heini Riitahuhta for Arabia, make up a collection of tableware including plates and bowls. Each pattern is designed to represent one of the four seasons: (from left to right) Spring Clock, Summer Ray (see opposite), Autumn Glow and Winter Star.

1

2

3

4

Transfer Pad Printing an Arabia Runo Mug

Featured company Arabia Finland www.arabia.fi

This printing process is a combination of rotary pad printing and transfer printing (see Decal printing, page 152). Each colour in the design is screen printed (page 116) (image **1**). Meanwhile, the raw ceramic is prepared with a durable transparent glaze (image **2**). The mugs are then fired for 20 hours and reach 1,260°C (2,300°F).

The pre-printed image is transferred from a decal onto the rotating silicone pad. A mug is mounted onto the rotating jig and spun against the silicone pad so the complete ink image is transferred perfectly on the surface of the glaze (image **3**).

The printed mugs are stacked (image **4**) ready for the second firing cycle. During this cycle the ink is drawn into the surface of the glaze just as in conventional pad printing. The pinkish varnish, which supports the ink during transfer, is burnt away during firing.

Hydro Transfer Printing

Hydro transfer printing is used to apply decorative finishes to 3D surfaces. A range of vivid graphics can be digitally printed onto the transfer film, which is wrapped around the product using water pressure. Any material that can be submerged in the water bath can be printed onto.

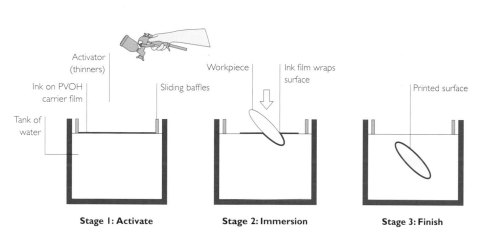

Activator
(thinners)

Ink on PVOH
carrier film

Tank of
water

Sliding baffles

Stage 1: Activate

Workpiece

Ink film wraps
surface

Stage 2: Immersion

Printed surface

Stage 3: Finish

Essential Information

VISUAL QUALITY	●●●●●○○○
SPEED	●●●●○○○○
SET-UP COST	●●○○○○○○
UNIT COST	●●●●●●○○
ENVIRONMENT	●●●●○○○○

Alternative and competing processes include:
- Dye Sublimation Printing
- Screen Printing
- Tampo Printing

What is Hydro Transfer Printing?

It is known by many different names, including immersion coating, cubic printing and aqua graphics. They are all basically the same process, but different companies supply the various printing technologies.

Prior to applying the print, the surface is prepared, typically by coating it with an opaque basecoat (primer).

The immersion process is carried out in a tank of warm water at 30°C to 40°C (86–104°F). The transfer film is made up of a polyvinyl alcohol (PVOH) backing and ink surface. In stage 1, the PVOH side is laid onto the surface of the warm water and triggered with a spray activator. Sliding baffles are used to keep it in place.

In stage 2, the part is immersed and the pressure of the water forces the ink to follow the contours of the surface. After printing, the inks are locked in with a transparent topcoat (lacquer). This is applied by spraying and can be matt or gloss depending on the application.

Notes for Designers

QUALITY The quality of print in this process is equal to digital printing and the colour range is limitless. The ink is made durable by sandwiching it between a basecoat (primer) and a topcoat (lacquer). Using spray coating will, however, affect the overall surface finish. For example, a gloss topcoat will gather along edges and around holes, resulting in visible welling which is known as fat edges.

TYPICAL APPLICATIONS This process is cost effective and is used to apply graphics onto the surface of automotive interiors (walnut dashboards, for example) mobile phone covers, computer mice, sunglasses and sports equipment.

COST AND SPEED There are no tooling costs. However, small parts will need to be mounted on specially designed jigs. Cycle time is typically no more than 10 minutes. Labour costs are moderate because the majority of applications are manually dipped.

MATERIALS Almost any hard material can be coated. If it can be spray painted, then it is also feasible to apply hydro transfer graphics.

ENVIRONMENTAL IMPACTS A variety of sprays, thinners and chemicals are used in the process. All contamination can be filtered from the water and disposed of safely.

A range of imitations and decorations With this process it is possible to make products look as if they are formed from materials that would be too expensive or impractical to use otherwise. There is a wide range of standard prints to choose from and it is also possible to print your own design. The standard range of hyper-realistic finishes includes patterns such as wood grain, camouflage, animal markings (for instance, snake skin) and carbon fibre. Alternatively, geometric patterns, flags, photographs or a company's own graphics can be applied for decorative effect.

1

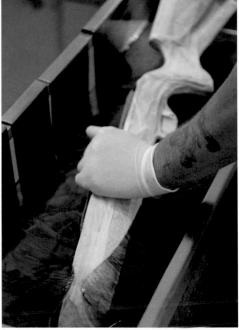

2

3

4

Case Study

Hydro Transfer Printing a Rifle Stock

Featured company Hydrographics
www.hydro-graphics.co.uk

The film (image **1**) is cut to length and floated on top of the warm water bath. Once the film has been activated, the part is carefully dipped into the tank (image **2**). Some parts can be printed in a single dip, others have to be masked and printed in several cycles. These parts are masked in two halves because there is a re-entrant angle on the trigger guard which cannot be printed well in a single dip.

It is immersed in the water at an angle that ensures no air bubbles form on its surface. The ink is gelatinous, but remains intact as it wraps around the 3D shape. The surface of the water is cleared before the product is brought out to avoid any contamination (image **3**).

The finished item (image **4**) shows how well the film conforms to the shape of the part because it is not distorted and has even filled small recesses and channels.

Finishing Techniques

3

Fill, Cap and Label

Packaging containers of many familiar household items, including drinks, cleaning products and cosmetics, are filled, capped and labelled by fully automated and high speed production lines. There are countless combinations of materials and processes to choose from depending on cost, volume and application.

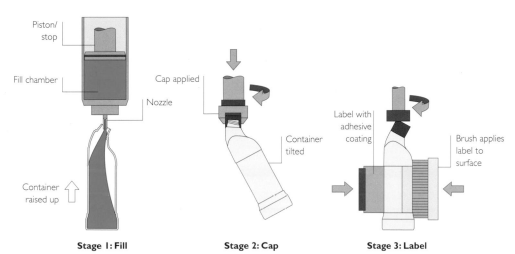

Piston/
stop

Fill chamber

Nozzle

Container
raised up

Stage 1: Fill

Cap applied

Container
tilted

Stage 2: Cap

Label with
adhesive
coating

Brush applies
label to
surface

Stage 3: Label

Essential Information

VISUAL QUALITY	●●●●●●●
SPEED	○○●●●●●
SET-UP COST	●●●●●●●
UNIT COST	○●●●●●●
ENVIRONMENT	○●●●●●●

Alternative and competing processes include:
• Plastic Welding
• Screen Printing

What is Filling, Capping and Labelling?

The bottles are often transferred directly from the production line to the filling station. In other cases, they are packaged and shipped to the factory where they will be filled, capped and labelled.

In stage 1, the bottles are raised up to meet the nozzle under the fill chamber. A predetermined measure of liquid, typically around 0.005–25 litres (0.18 fl. oz. to 6 gallons), is transferred into the hollow container by gravity. Materials that do not flow so easily, such as mayonnaise, are forced into the container by a piston.

In stage 2, a cap is fixed in place by screwing, pressing or corking. If the neck is not vertical then the bottle is tilted to accommodate the angle. In stage 3, the label is bonded to the outside surface. Adhesive is applied to the label and it is smoothed onto the container by a soft brush as the container rotates 360°.

QUALITY The final quality of the packaging is determined by the choice of forming process, such as glassblowing (page 28) or plastic blow molding (page 34), the method of capping or stopping and the choice of materials and printing process for the label.

TYPICAL APPLICATIONS These processes are used to fill and finish all household, medical, industrial and other rigid packages containing liquids, such as drinks, medicines, cleaning fluids and cosmetics.

COST AND SPEED Tooling costs are moderate to high and depend on the level of automation. Cycle time is very rapid and ranges from 15 to 400 containers per minute. Labour costs are relatively low, although manual operations increase the costs.

MATERIALS All liquid and free-flowing materials can be packaged in this way. Containers that are filled are typically manufactured in plastic, glass, ceramic or metal.

ENVIRONMENTAL IMPACTS There is very little waste created in operation. The full environmental impacts are a culmination of all the processes and materials involved, including forming and printing. Combining dissimilar materials can create problems during recycling.

Self-adhesive labels These labels were flexography printed by Colchester Print Group (page 133). Since a wide range of materials can be utilized this technique is used to print the majority of packaging labels. Examples include self-adhesive, paper, plastic and metalized film. The labels are printed and die cut on the backing film in a continuous process.

1

2

Case Study

Filling, Capping and Labelling a Cleaning Liquid Container

Featured company Polimoon Packaging
www.polimoon.com

These plastic containers were formed by extrusion blow molding (EBM) (page 34). Prior to filling, each container is pressure tested (image **1**) to ensure that it is watertight. Each container is then brought in line with the fill chamber where an exact measure of liquid is fed in through the nozzle by gravity (image **2**). Each bottle makes a complete journey around the circular filling station, after which it is full. The cap is screwed onto the bottle (image **3**) and a label bonded in place (image **4**). Operating speeds can be as fast as 400 containers per minute, although this is usually slowed down by the rate of filling.

3

4

Vacuum Metalizing

Vacuum metalizing is used to coat materials with a bright metallic layer of pure aluminium. It can be coloured to produce the look and feel of a range of metals, such as chrome, silver and gold. It is used for high-end packaging and striking displays.

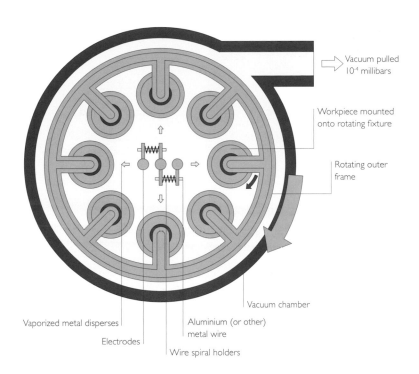

Vacuum pulled 10⁻⁴ millibars

Workpiece mounted onto rotating fixture

Rotating outer frame

Vacuum chamber

Vaporized metal disperses

Aluminium (or other) metal wire

Electrodes

Wire spiral holders

Essential Information

VISUAL QUALITY	●●●●●●●○
SPEED	●●●●●○○○
SET-UP COST	●●●●●●○○
UNIT COST	●●●●●○○○
ENVIRONMENT	●●●●●●○○

Alternative and competing processes include:
• Pad Printing
• Screen Printing
• Spray Printing

What is Vacuum Metalizing?

The workpieces are mounted onto rotating holding fixtures (custom made for each part), which are, in turn, rotated on spinning wheels. The assembly is suspended within a frame, which also rotates. All in all, the parts are rotated around three parallel axes simultaneously to ensure an even coating with line-of-sight geometry.

A vacuum is generated within the metalizing chamber and then an electrical discharge is passed through the aluminium (or other metal) wire by the electrodes. The combination of the electric current and high vacuum cause the almost pure metal to vaporize in an instant. It bursts into a plume of metal vapour, which condenses on the relatively cool surface of the workpiece.

Notes for Designers

QUALITY Vacuum metalizing increases surface quality and colouring capability. However, the highly reflective layer will show up any imperfections in the substrate.

TYPICAL APPLICATIONS Most metallic-looking plastic products are finished in this way, for instance, cosmetics packaging and phone accessories. Vacuum metalizing is utilized to produce metallic graphics, such as silver logos, on products.

COST AND SPEED There are no tooling costs. Cycle time is moderate (up to six hours). It is quite a labour intensive process: the parts have to be sprayed, loaded, unloaded and sprayed again.

MATERIALS Many materials can be coated, including metals, rigid and flexible plastics, composites, ceramics and glass. Natural fibres are generally not suitable: it is very difficult to apply a vacuum if moisture is present.

ENVIRONMENTAL IMPACTS This process creates very little waste. Spraying the basecoat and topcoat has an impact equivalent to spray painting.

Coloured vacuum metalizing (left) Applying a translucent tinted topcoat onto the aluminium produces vivid colours. Relatively inexpensive plastic parts can be coated and coloured to look like metals such as anodized aluminium, copper or gold.

Cosmetics packaging (above) Injection-molded (page 52) packaging for premium cosmetics, such as perfume caps and face cream containers, is made to look like bright chrome using vacuum metalizing.

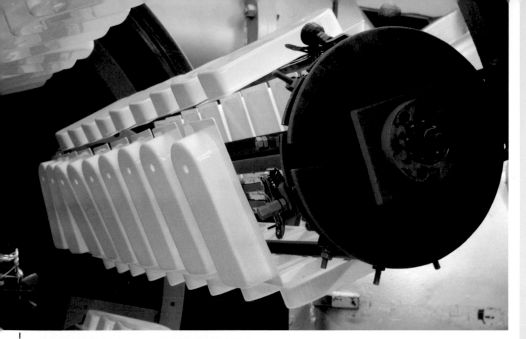

1

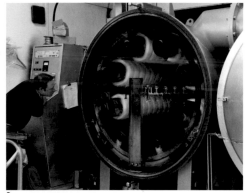

2

3

4

Metalizing Point-of-sale Displays

Featured company VMC Limited
www.vmclimited.co.uk

These point-of-sale parts are formed by vacuum forming (page 56). They are mounted onto jigs, sprayed with a basecoat and loaded onto the rotating holding fixtures (image **1**).

The wire spiral holders that connect the positive and negative electrodes are loaded with a charge of aluminium wire (image **2**) and the whole assembly is loaded into the vacuum chamber. The operator checks the spinning jigs (image **3**) and the vacuum chamber is sealed shut with the parts inside.

Once a sufficient vacuum is reached an electrical discharge is passed through the wire, causing the aluminium to vaporize and coat all the surfaces. The parts are removed from the chamber (image **4**) and sprayed with a yellow topcoat to produce a durable gold coloured finish (image **5**).

5

Flocking

Short and densely packed fibres are bonded to the surface of the workpiece, standing on end, to create a soft and vividly coloured finish that feels like velvet. Flocking is used to create a distinctive look and feel on packaging, point-of-sale and graphic applications.

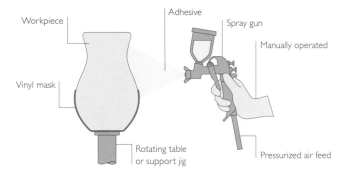

Stage 1: Applying adhesive

Workpiece

Adhesive

Spray gun

Manually operated

Vinyl mask

Rotating table
or support jig

Pressurized air feed

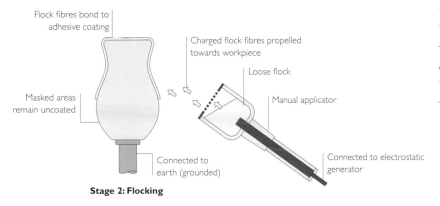

Stage 2: Flocking

Flock fibres bond to
adhesive coating

Charged flock fibres propelled
towards workpiece

Loose flock

Masked areas
remain uncoated

Manual applicator

Connected to
earth (grounded)

Connected to electrostatic
generator

Essential Information

VISUAL QUALITY	●●●●●●●●
SPEED	●●●●●●●
SET-UP COST	●●●●●●●
UNIT COST	●●●●●●●●
ENVIRONMENT	●●●●●●●●

Related processes include:
- Masked Flocking
- Masking

Alternative and competing processes include:
- Screen Printing

What is Flocking?

In stage 1, areas that are not to be coated are protected with a mask. This is typically made by vinyl cutting (page 108). Then the entire surface is coated with a conductive adhesive, which is built up to a sufficient thickness to support the fibres once they are applied.

In stage 2, the mask is removed and the workpiece is grounded. Flocking is an electrostatic process: the fibres are charged with high voltage – 40,000–80,000 volts, depending on the application – as they leave

the applicator. This potential difference draws the fibres towards the surface of the grounded workpiece where they penetrate the layer of adhesive and stand perpendicular to the surface.

As the surface is gradually covered, the fibres are drawn to the areas that have the greatest electrical energy. This ensures that a dense and even coating is built up. The fibres are permanently bonded in place.

Notes for Designers

QUALITY Colour is rich, uniform and matt. The softness varies according to the type and length of the fibre.

TYPICAL APPLICATIONS Flocking is used to decorate packaging and point-of-sale displays. Graphic applications are diverse, such as book covers, posters and even the walls of exhibitions.

COST AND SPEED There are no tooling costs, although jigs may be required. Cycle time depends on the size of the part and curing time of the adhesive. Labour costs are moderate for low-volume parts. High-volume applications are typically automated.

MATERIALS Polyamide (PA) nylon is the most common flocking fibre, but it is possible to flock with other synthetic and natural fibres from 0.2–10 mm (0.0079– 0.4 in.) in length. Almost any material can be flocked.

ENVIRONMENTAL IMPACTS Chemicals are used and dust is produced during flocking, so suitable facemasks and breathing equipment are required. Flock cannot be recycled. The surface finish can last for many years, depending on application, and it is possible to retouch damaged coatings.

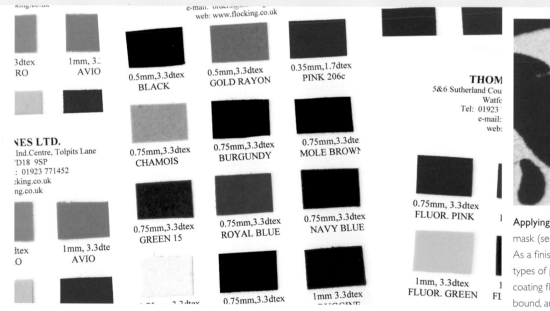

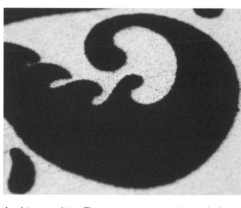

Colour swatches Flock is available in almost any colour. Mixing different colours and lengths is possible: for example, a composite flock is used to mimic animal fur or fruit skin, such as kiwis, for packaging.

Applying graphics The pattern created using a vinyl mask (see opposite) has very good edge definition. As a finishing process, it can be combined with all other types of printing and forming. It is equally suitable for coating flat parts, such as book covers before they are bound, and 3D, such as cosmetics packaging.

Case Study

Masking and Flocking a Graphic Design

Featured company Thomas & Vines Ltd
www.flocking.co.uk

To apply graphics accurately a vinyl cut mask is used for the glue application. First, the vinyl is rubbed down onto the surface to be flocked (image **1**). Suitable adhesive is mixed with pigment so it will not be visible beneath the flock, then poured into the spray gun (image **2**).

The surface is sprayed with adhesive and the mask is carefully removed (image **3**). Electric pink nylon fibres are loaded into the applicator (image **4**). The fibres are positively charged as they leave the applicator, which propels them towards the surface of the electrically grounded workpiece (image **5**). A dense flock coating is achieved within a few minutes.

1

2

3

4

5

Embossing and Debossing

Embossed and debossed profiles are formed in sheet materials with heated metal tools. Pressure is applied to form an indent, known as deboss, or a raised surface profile, known as emboss. It is often used in conjunction with foil blocking; on unprinted paper it is known as blind embossing.

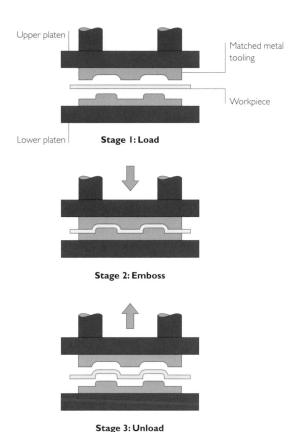

Upper platen

Matched metal tooling

Workpiece

Lower platen

Stage 1: Load

Stage 2: Emboss

Stage 3: Unload

Essential Information

VISUAL QUALITY	●●●●●●●●
SPEED	●●●●●●●
SET-UP COST	●●●●●●
UNIT COST	●●●●●●
ENVIRONMENT	●●●●●●

Related processes include:
- Metal Embossing
- Paper Embossing

Alternative and competing processes include:
- Foil Blocking
- Metal Press Forming
- Varnishing
- Vinyl Cutting

What is Embossing?

On paper, leather and textiles, foil blocking (page 186) and embossing are essentially the same process. The difference is that with foil blocking a layer of foil is placed between the tool and substrate during stamping. In each process, heat and pressure are applied.

Embossing is carried out between matched tooling, whereas debossing only requires an impression tool. Embossing tools have a small radius at the perimeter of the design for aesthetic and functional reasons: a sharp edge would stress paper fibres, for example. Where foil blocking and embossing are combined the foil cut-off is not as clean as in separate operations. This is because the tooling is very slightly different. Foil blocking is carried out on the face of the material with a square edge tool, whereas embossing tooling has a small radius and the best results are achieved when pressing from the opposite side into a matched tool.

Notes for Designers

QUALITY The quality depends on the material and the tools. Matched tooling is used to produce high quality and long-lasting profiles in paper. Thicker materials tend to emboss better because they are self-supporting.

TYPICAL APPLICATIONS High quality printed materials including books, stationery and packaging. It is also used in metal packaging such as aluminium cans (page 46), tinplate cans and packaging (page 44).

COST AND SPEED Tooling costs are low to moderate depending on the material. Cycle time is rapid: up to 1,000 parts per hour can be pressed. Labour costs are low.

MATERIALS Materials that will stretch without breaking, such as paper, leather and metal, can be embossed and debossed. With the addition of steam, it is possible to form thin sheets of timber, such as veneer, permanently.

ENVIRONMENTAL IMPACTS Environmental impact is low. This process does not produce any waste, but a little heat is used in operation.

Mario Bellini These business cards, designed by Alexander Åhnebrink, are blind embossed in heavy paper stock. Forming the paper between metal tools at high pressure reproduces the intricate details of Mario's handwriting.

Branded wood The text and logo are applied to this Great Wall Chinese wine box by debossing with a hot metal tool. Heavier debossing and branding are achieved by increasing the temperature and pressure applied.

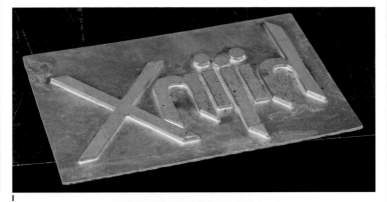

1

Blind Embossing

Featured company Modern Activity
www.modernactivity.co.uk

Embossing is used to create subtle
and high quality effects on printed and
unprinted sheet materials. The tooling
(image **1**), which is machined from metal,
is placed into a press and pre-heated.

When unprinted materials are used, as
in this case, it is known as blind embossing.
The paper is loaded into the press (image
2) and vertical force is applied (image **3**).

The material is perfectly formed with
a debossed graphic (image **4**) which
is a mirror image of the metal tool.
This is a rapid and repeatable process
used a great deal in the packaging and
printing industries and suitable for both
small and high-volume production runs.

2

3

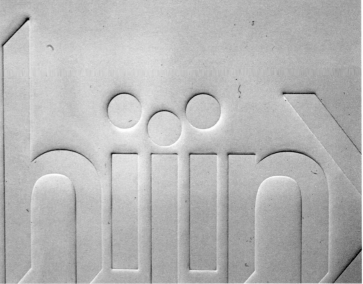

4

What is Metal Embossing?

In practice, metal embossing is shallow metal press forming (page 42). The process is carried out on a punch press using matched tooling.

The metal blank is loaded onto the lower tool. The punch clamps and forms the part in a single stroke. The stripper rises up to remove the part after pressing.

Sometimes the part is formed in a continuous strip and many sheet-metal processes are carried out in sequence to form the part. This is the norm in very high-volume production.

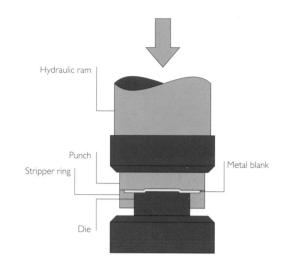

Hydraulic ram

Punch

Stripper ring

Die

Metal blank

Press forming Metal press forming and embossing are essentially the same process. Therefore, they can be carried out simultaneously if all of the operations are in the same line of draw (i.e., there are not any undercuts). This metal lid, used to seal a card tube containing a bottle of whisky, has been punched, stamped (page 42) and embossed from a pre-printed sheet in a single operation.

1

2

Case Study

Embossing a Biscuit Tin

Featured company Massilly   www.massilly.com

Sheets of tinplate (tin-coated steel) are prepared by printing (see offset lithography printing, page 124) and cutting to size. The stacked parts (image **1**) are ready to be embossed. In this case they are embossed individually and by hand (image **2**). Despite this, it is a rapid process.

Matched tooling produces a debossed profile on the back face (image **3**). This ensures a very high quality embossing on the front face (image **4**). The registration between the print and the embossing is very precise and repeatable because the metal is stiff and so can be accurately registered in the tool.

This part will form the body of a biscuit tin (page 45).

3

4

Foil Blocking

Foil blocking is a dry process used to apply decorative finishes to a range of materials, including paper, wood and leather. A profiled metal tool is pressed onto the surface of the part and leaves behind a relief impression in combination with a reverse image in foil.

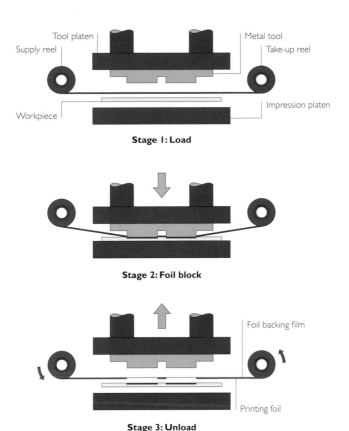

Tool platen
Supply reel
Metal tool
Take-up reel
Impression platen
Workpiece

Stage 1: Load

Stage 2: Foil block

Foil backing film

Printing foil

Stage 3: Unload

Essential Information

VISUAL QUALITY	●●●●●● ○ ●
SPEED	●●●●●● ○ ●
SET-UP COST	●●●●●●●
UNIT COST	●●●●●●●
ENVIRONMENT	●●●●●●●

Alternative and competing processes include:
- Pad Printing
- Screen Printing
- Varnishing and Laminating
- Vinyl Cutting

What is Foil Blocking?

Several terms are used to describe foil blocking, including hot stamping, hot foiling and foil embossing.

The raised areas of the metal tool apply the image. They can be linear or rotary in orientation: rotary processes are very rapid and can be used for continuous production of sheet materials and cylindrical parts.

The tools are heated to between 100°C and 200°C (212–392°F). The combination of heat and pressure bond the foil to the workpiece on contact. It is embedded into the surface, and the depth of impression is determined by the hardness of the materials and the pressure applied to the tool. The tool has square edges, which helps to provide a clean edge on the cut-out.

Notes for Designers

QUALITY A benefit of foil is that it is opaque and so registration is not usually as critical as with other materials. Even so, the metal tooling can be set up to precise requirements. A slight impression is formed on the surface of the material. Thin materials will emboss all the way through and so have a raised surface on the reverse.

TYPICAL APPLICATIONS This process is used a great deal in the printing industry to decorate book covers, packaging, invitations, flyers, posters, CD cases and corporate stationery.

COST AND SPEED Tooling costs are very low. Rotary tools and matched tooling are more expensive. Cycle time is rapid: up to 1,000 parts per hour can be processed. Labour costs are low.

MATERIALS Most materials can be foil blocked, including leather, textile, wood, paper, card and plastic.

ENVIRONMENTAL IMPACTS Environmental impacts are low. Recycling used foil is impractical, so some designs, such as borders, waste all of the foil within the design area.

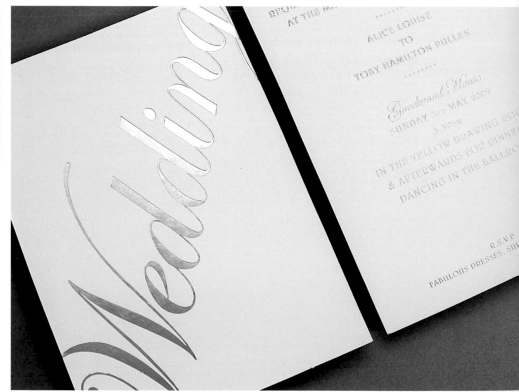

Foils (above) There are many different types of foil. They are supplied on rolls and are backed onto thin polyester film. On the surface of the foil is a thin film of adhesive that bonds it to the substrate when separated by heat and pressure from the polyester backing film. For solid colours it is possible to colour match using a reference such as Pantone.

Wedding invitations (right) Designed by Campbell Hay for the Pullens' wedding in 2009, this example is metallic gold. This process is suitable for all scales of manufacture, including prototyping, low-volume and mass-production.

1

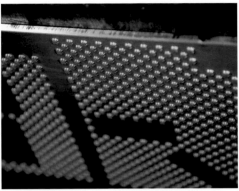

2

3

4

Case Study

Gold Foil Blocking

Featured company Impressions Foil Ltd
www.impressionsfoiling.co.uk

A sheet of paper is picked up by a series of vacuum nozzles, which feed it into the printer (image **1**). The metal tool is mounted onto the press behind the foil (images **2** and **3**). Each piece of paper is fed onto the impression bed and the pressing takes less than a second (image **4**). Platen letterpress machines, like this one, are used for relatively low-volume production of invitations, cards and flyers. The reflective gold foil is reproduced accurately on the surface of the card (image **5**).

5

Varnishing and Laminating

Varnish is a clear liquid coating applied to a printed material. It is known as spot varnishing when it is applied to specific areas only. Laminating is the process of bonding a film of plastic onto the page. Both are used to decorate and protect the printed surface.

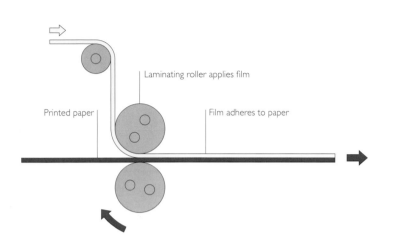

Printed paper

Laminating roller applies film

Film adheres to paper

Essential Information

VISUAL QUALITY	●●●●●●●●
SPEED	●●●●●●●●
SET-UP COST	●●●●●●●●
UNIT COST	●●●●●●●●
ENVIRONMENT	●●●●●●●●

Related processes include:
• Spot Varnish
• Varnishing and Laminating

Alternative and competing processes include:
• Foil Blocking

What is Varnishing and Laminating?

Varnish is applied by printing and can be carried out in-line – by offset lithography (page 124) and flexography (page 130) – or as a secondary process by screen printing (page 116). A similar effect to spot varnishing can be achieved by foil blocking a clear foil (page 186).

The colourless liquid is applied to the surface of printed material. Formulations cured with ultraviolet (UV) light give the best results. It is known as overprint varnish or full bleed when applied evenly all over and a spot varnish when applied to specific areas only.

Laminating is separate from printing and used to cover the entire page with a thin film of plastic. Heat and pressure bond the materials together. The end product is a composite of paper and plastic and therefore more difficult to recycle.

It is possible to combine the processes, for instance, applying a gloss spot varnish onto a matt laminate for maximum visual impact.

Notes for Designers

QUALITY Adding lamination or varnish improves the durability of printed materials. Finishes include gloss, satin, neutral, matt and textured. A gloss finish will improve colour saturation and matt will reduce glare and soften colour. Lamination is the most durable and resistant to wear, moisture and even tearing.

TYPICAL APPLICATIONS Applications are widespread and include stationery, labels, packaging, magazines, postcards, photographs and book covers. In fact, the cover of this book is laminated with a gloss film for added protection.

COST AND SPEED Tooling costs are low, especially if the process is carried out in-line. Cycle time is rapid and labour costs are low.

MATERIALS The range of plastic laminating films includes clear, coloured, textured, holographic and iridescent. Varnishes are clear.

ENVIRONMENTAL IMPACTS Varnishing does not affect the impact of the printed material significantly. However, laminated materials are more difficult to recycle. This is important for disposable products such as packaging.

Spot varnish The printed areas on this perfect bound book cover are spot varnished with a gloss finish. It is carried out in-line using offset lithography printing (page 124). The change in texture helps the green text to stand out against the white background.

Case Study

Laminating a Folder

Featured company Colchester Print Group
www.brecklandprint.com

Clear matt laminating film (image **1**)
is used to protect the folder cover from
wear and tear in application. The cover
(image **2**) is printed using offset lithography
(page 124).

Each page is loaded into the laminating
press. They slightly overlap so that
they form a continuous strip (image **3**).
The plastic film and paper are pressed
together and heated to create a strong
bond. The laminated pages pass between
tension rollers (image **4**) to de-stress the
composite and reduce warpage and other
defects that occur as a result of laminating.

Finally the pages are stacked (image **5**).
They are ready to be die cut to size and
constructed (page 79).

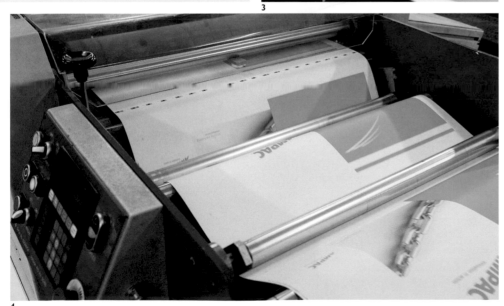

Binding

Binding is the process of assembling and finishing the pages, inserts and covers in the construction of books, magazines and catalogues. Many types of sheet material, such as paper, board, felt and plastic, can be bound within rigid or flexible covers using a range of techniques.

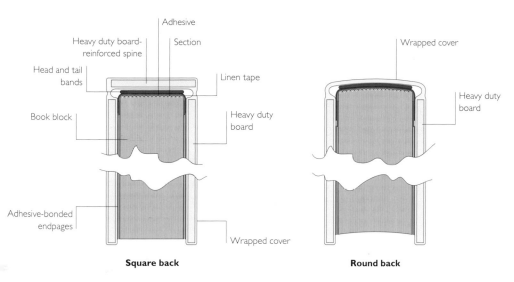

Head and tail bands
Heavy duty board-reinforced spine
Adhesive
Section
Linen tape
Heavy duty board
Book block
Adhesive-bonded endpages
Wrapped cover

Square back

Wrapped cover
Heavy duty board

Round back

Essential Information

VISUAL QUALITY	● ● ● ● ● ● ● ●
SPEED	● ● ● ○ ● ● ● ○
SET-UP COST	○ ● ● ● ● ● ● ○
UNIT COST	● ● ● ● ● ● ● ○
ENVIRONMENT	○ ● ● ● ● ● ● ●

Related processes include:
- Case Binding or Hardback
- Paperback
- Saddle Stitching
- Spiral Binding and Canadian Binding

Alternative and competing processes include:
- Plastic Welding

What is Case Binding?

Used to assemble what are known as hardback, hardcover or hardbound books, case binding is the process of binding with rigid covers. The heavy duty board is typically encased with paper, cloth or leather. In some cases this is covered with a printed dust jacket.

The book block consists of sections, which are produced by folding a large signature (printed sheet) and cutting it to size. The extent of books bound in this way is divisible by the number of pages in a section, which is typically 4, 8, 16 or 32. The sections are sewn (thread stitched or section sewn) or glued (burst binding) together and the spine is reinforced with linen tape and adhesive. The head and tail bands protect the ends of the binding and the cover is joined to the book block using endpapers.

There are two main types of case binding: square back or round back. Before modern binding techniques, a round back was used to compensate for the additional thickness of the sections caused by thread sewing.

Notes for Designers

QUALITY Sewn bindings can be laid flat because they are not restricted by the depth of glue in the spine; case bindings are more durable than paperbacks.

TYPICAL APPLICATIONS Books are either casebound or paperback, whereas magazines and catalogues are perfect bound or saddle stitched. Spiral binding and Canadian binding (additional protective cover) are low cost and used for one-off publications and low volumes.

COST AND SPEED Tooling costs are low. Cycle time is moderate and depends on the quality, volume and level of automation. Labour costs are low to high, depending on the type of binding required.

MATERIALS Typically, the text block is paper-based and the covers are paper, board and/or linen. However, it is possible to use any practical sheet material – such as wood, metal, plastic and felt – but this will increase the costs.

ENVIRONMENTAL IMPACTS The environmental impact is low, although combining different materials will make it more difficult to recycle.

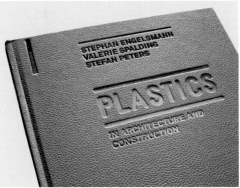

Types of binding (far left) This stack includes books that are (from top to bottom): a section-sewn paperback; spiral-bound with a hard cover; section-sewn hardback with a square back and dust jacket; section-sewn without a cover; perfect bound; flexibound; section-sewn paperback; section-sewn hardback with a round back; section-sewn hardback with a square back; and section-sewn hardback with a round back.

Decorating the cover (above, left) The textured and pearlescent cover of *Plastics*, published by Birkhäuser in 2010, is foil blocked (page 186) with iridescent film. All types of printing and decoration can be applied to covers, including flocking (page 176), die cutting (page 76), embossing (page 180) and even laser cutting (page 104).

Round back (left) The spine of hardback book blocks is stitched and glued together, but it is separate from the case. Compared to binding techniques that bond the book block spine directly to the case, this is more durable and means the spreads can be opened wider and therefore flatter.

Case Study

A Section-sewn Hardback

Featured company RS Bookbinders Ltd
www.rsbookbinders.co.uk

In this case, the book is made up of 16-page sections (image **1**), which consist of a large signature (printed sheet) folded 4 times and cut to size on a guillotine. Each section is sewn through the centrefold and joined to the adjacent section. Linen tape is adhesive bonded onto the sewn edges of the sections and the assembly is cut to size (image **2**). This produces a neat edge (image **3**). Head and tail bands have not been used in this example. The hard covers are made up of heavy duty grey board which is 2.5 mm (0.1 in.) thick and concealed in paper (image **4**). Decorations, such as foil blocking (page 186) and die cutting (page 76), are applied prior to assembly. The cover is adhesive-bonded to the endpapers, the assembly is clamped in a press and the adhesive cures (image **5**).

1

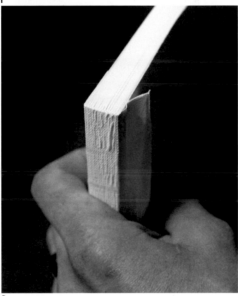

2

3

4

5

What is Paperback Binding?

The two main types of adhesive bonded paperback are perfect bound and section bound. The third type of paperback is flexibound, which is how the *Manufacturing Guides* are bound. Flexibound is more durable because it is made using the same elements as case binding (page 195) apart from the heavy duty card. In other words, the spine is strengthened with linen tape and head and tail bands, and is not bonded to the book block.

Section bindings are made up of groups of pages sewn or adhesive-bonded together into sections. The spine,

the first and the last page are bonded directly into the cover to hold the assembly in place. Section-sewn bindings are more durable.

In the case of perfect binding, individual pages are bonded directly into the cover. Used to produce catalogues and journals, for example, it is the least expensive and least durable binding method. Adhesive is soaked up the edge of the pages to increase the bond area and strength. As a result, the pages will not lie flat in the same way that section bound editions will.

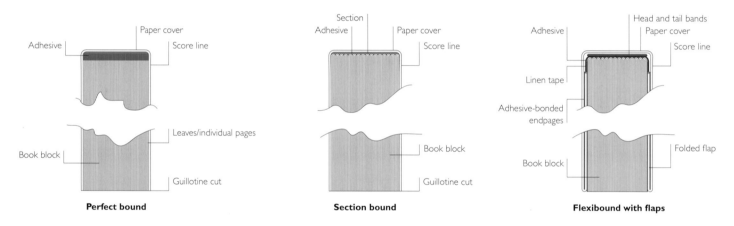

Perfect bound

Adhesive · Paper cover · Score line · Book block · Leaves/individual pages · Guillotine cut

Section bound

Section · Adhesive · Paper cover · Score line · Book block · Guillotine cut

Flexibound with flaps

Adhesive · Head and tail bands · Paper cover · Score line · Linen tape · Adhesive-bonded endpages · Book block · Folded flap

Perforated knife fold (far left) The spine of this folded section has been perforated for burst binding. This allows the adhesive to penetrate deeper into the spine and increases the strength of non-sewn section binding.

Folding (left) Folded assemblies can be used with all types of binding. This Miss Selfridge press book, created by Hawaii Design, is made up of 8-page double gatefolds. Each spread opens to 4-page widths. Folds are either created in-line (see what is folding and saddle stitching?, page 200), or during die cutting (page 76).

1

2

Case Study

Perfect Binding a Paperback

Featured company RS Bookbinders Ltd
www.rsbookbinders.co.uk

Perfect binding joins the individual pages to the cover with adhesive. The book block is clamped together (image **1**) and adhesive is applied along the spine and onto around 3 mm (0.118 in.) of the face of each page. This ensures good bond strength and stops the pages being pulled out too easily during use. The durability is therefore determined by the strength of the adhesive.

The book block is laid into the cover (image **2**), which has been scored to fold around the thickness of the pages and ensure a snug fit (image **3**). The pinch, where the cover folds, is away from the spine to reduce stress on the adhesive. The edges are trimmed using a guillotine (image **4**) to create a neat edge. The binding is finished (image **5**).

3

4

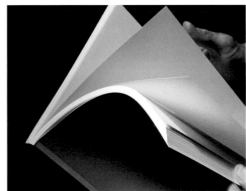

5

What is Folding and Saddle Stitching?

Folds are formed between two nip rolls. Either the paper is fed into the rolls by a knife, which produces a very sharp fold, or it is buckled in under pressure (known as buckle folding).

Saddle stitching is a simple and cost effective method for binding folded pages (folios) together. It is used in-line for high volumes of magazines and catalogues, for example.

A length of wire is cut to length and punched through the spine of the gathered folios. The total thickness of the spine is determined by the paper stock (or other material) and the number of folios to be combined. This sets the length of wire that is required for a secure binding. It is suitable for up to around 80 pages and the total number of pages (including front and back) will be divisible by 4.

It is possible to bind all types of different material using saddle stitching, but this may mean the process cannot be carried out in-line.

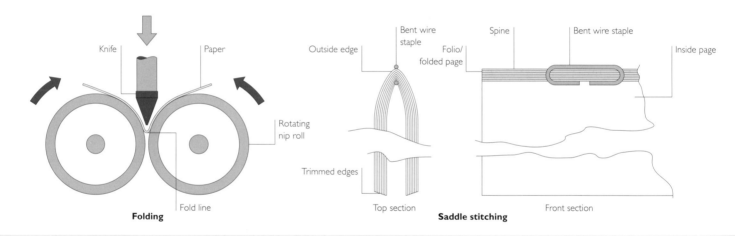

Folding

Saddle stitching

Folded and saddle stitched Circular steel wire is the most common staple material. It is resilient and strengthens when bent to form a staple. This is known as work hardening. Staples can also be produced from coated metals and copper, for example.

Case Study

Folding and Saddle Stitching a Catalogue

Featured company Colchester Print Group
www.brecklandprint.com

The offset lithography printed sheets (page 124) of this catalogue are guided through a slitter, which cuts them to the correct width (image **1**). It is more cost effective to carry out the entire trimming prior to binding. This results in a slightly staggered edge because the spine is folded in a single section.

After slitting, the pages are folded (image **2**). They are passed through a backbone-folding machine, which lines up the spine and clenches the page together to form a folio. Each folio is loaded onto the previous one in a continuous process. Each complete assembly passes through the saddle-stitching machine, which cuts the wire to length and punches it through the spine, clamping it tightly (image **3**).

The finished catalogues are loaded into shipping boxes (image **4**).

Glossary of Useful Terms and Abbreviations

Aniline dye
A synthetic dye used in flexographic inks (page 130).

Antique paper
A standard grade of paper with a rough uncoated finish.

Art board
Uncoated board.

Art paper
A high quality paper that contains mineral fillers. It is used especially for high quality, gloss and colour printing.

Bat
See decal.

Blind embossing
The process of embossing, debossing or die stamping unprinted materials (page 180).

Brightener
Fluorescing dye added to paper to make it appear a brighter white.

CAD
Computer-aided design (CAD) is a general term used to cover computer programmes that assist with engineering and 3D design.

Cardboard
A range of wood pulp-based sheet materials used for printing and packaging.

Carton board
Thin, flexible and resilient boards used in the production of cartons and boxes (see carton construction, page 82).

Cast-coated paper
A high gloss finish on paper stock obtained by pressing the wet coated paper against a polished drum during production.

Chromo paper
This stock has a waterproof China clay coating applied onto one side. It is high quality, available as matt or gloss and is typically used for labels and packaging.

CMYK
The four process colours, cyan, magenta, yellow and ketone, are collectively abbreviated as CMYK.

CNC
Machining equipment operated by a computer is known as computer numerical control (CNC). The number of operational axes determines the types of geometries that can be achieved. CNC engraving (page 86) is typically carried out on a 3-axis machine.

Copperplate printing
The process of using a plate of copper, engraved with a design, for printing. In the past it was used to print decals for decorating ceramics (see decal printing, page 152).

CTP
The process of transferring a design directly from the computer onto a plate-making machine is known as computer to plate (CTP). This has almost entirely eliminated traditional plate-making techniques, which are time-consuming, high cost and require a highly skilled operator. As a result, CTP has revolutionized offset lithography (page 124), flexography (page 130)

and rotogravure (page 134). It is more precise and faster, which results in higher quality prints and more cost effective pre-press.

Deboss
A recess impression made in the surface of a material. See also emboss.

Decal
Also know as a bat, this is the transfer medium used in the decoration of ceramics (see decal printing, page 152).

Densitometer
An instrument used to measure the density of colour. In printing it is used to measure the quality and consistency of printing using the colour calibration bars that run along the sides of printed material (image 5, page 127).

dpi
Dots per inch (dpi) is the measurement of resolution of an output device, such as a printer or a computer monitor.

DTP
Direct to plate, which is another term for CTP.

Duotone
A two-tone image produced using two-colour printing.

Dye
A coloured liquid that is added to ink to improve colour by absorbing visible light. See also pigment.

Dye sublimation
This describes the process of dyes transferring between two surfaces without melting (see dye sublimation printing, page 148 and decal printing, page 152).

Emboss
A relief impression made on the surface of a material. See also deboss.

EPS
Expanded polystyrene (PS).

Greyboard
A grey coloured board made from recycled materials. It is used for packaging and mounting applications.

Half tone
A method of producing continuous tone images using patterns of dots (see image, page 15).

Intaglio
The opposite of relief printing: ink is transferred onto the paper or other material from engraved recesses in the surface of the print plate.

Lacquer
A high gloss coating applied to printed materials. See also varnish.

Mechanical paper
Grades of wood pulp-based paper that tend to yellow over time.

Pigment
Powder materials that are mixed with ink to add colour by absorbing visible light. There are many types and the quality and consistency will vary according to the source. See also dye.

Process colour
See CMYK.

Proof
A hardcopy print that is used to check colour, alignment and design before setting up for full-scale printing.

Registration
Aligning colours in the printing process.

Relief printing
Processes that apply ink onto the paper or other sheet material from raised areas on the surface of the tool. See also intaglio.

RIP
Raster image processor (RIP) software converts data from graphics files (fonts and graphics) into commands that are understood by the printer.

Special colour
See spot colour.

Spot colour
A special colour that cannot be achieved by mixing CMYK, such as metallic, fluorescent, thermochromatic or a very specific shade.

Spot varnish
The application of varnish to specific areas on a sheet of paper (page 192).

Stock
Paper or other fibre-based material that can be printed on.

Substrate
Any sheet material that can be printed on, such as metal, plastic and paper.

Thermoplastic
A polymeric material that becomes soft and pliable when heated. It can be shaped and re-shaped by a range of molding processes such as injection molding (page 52).

Uncoated wood-free paper
General purpose paper.

Varnish
A clear or tinted liquid coating applied on top of printed materials. It is available in gloss, satin or matt finishes.

Directory of Featured Companies

Albemarle Graphics Limited
35 Astbury Road
London SE15 2NL
United Kingdom
www.ag-online.co.uk

Alexander Åhnebrink Design
Via Giovanni Ventura 3
20134 Milano
Italy
www.ahnebrink.com

Alexir Partnership
Enterprise Way
Edenbridge
Kent TN8 6HF
United Kingdom
www.alexir.co.uk

Arabia Finland
Fiskars Home
PO Box 130
Hämeentie 135
FIN-00561 Helsinki
Finland
www.arabia.fi

Ashford Mouldings
The Plasticom Group
Hilton Road
Cobbs Wood Industrial Estate
Ashford
Kent TN23 1EW
United Kingdom
www.ukplasticmouldings.co.uk

Aspect Signs & Engraving
Unit A5, Bounds Green Industrial
Estate
Ring Way
London N11 2UD
United Kingdom
www.aspect-signs.co.uk

Ball Packaging Europe
Kaiserswerther Straße 115
40880 Ratingen
Germany
www.ball-europe.com

Beatson Clark
The Glass Works
Greasbrough Road
Rotherham
South Yorkshire S60 1TZ
United Kingdom
www.beatsonclark.co.uk

Campbell Hay
Lion House
3 Plough Yard
London EC2A 3LP
United Kingdom
www.campbellhay.com

Colchester Print Group
Haverscroft Industrial Estate
New Road
Attleborough
Norfolk NR17 1YE
United Kingdom
www.brecklandprint.com

Cullen Packaging
10 Dawsholm Avenue
Dawsholm Industrial Estate
Glasgow G20 0TS
United Kingdom
www.cullen.co.uk

Cyril Luff Metal Decorators Ltd
57–58 Springvale Industrial Estate
Cwmbran
Gwent NP44 5BD
United Kingdom
www.cyrilluff.co.uk

Designersblock
32 Cremer Street
London E2 8HD
United Kingdom
www.verydesignersblock.com

ENL Limited
Unit 6–8, Victory Trading Estate
Kiln Road
Portsmouth
Hampshire PO3 5LP
United Kingdom
www.enl.co.uk

Felthams
Cawood Close (off Estover
Road)
March
Cambridgeshire PE15 8SF
United Kingdom
www.cplfelthams.co.uk

Gavin Coyle
20 High Street
London N8 7PB
United Kingdom
www.gavincoyle.co.uk

Global Vacuum Forming Ltd
Vedonis Works
Leicester Road
Lutterworth
Leicester LE17 4HD
United Kingdom
www.gvf.co.uk

Greece is for Lovers
13A Karyatidon Str.
Athens 117 42
Greece
www.greeceisforlovers.com

Hawaii Design
3rd Floor, 2A Luke Street
London EC2A 4NT
United Kingdom
www.hawaiidesign.co.uk

Hydrographics
Unit 4, Brockett Park Industrial
Estate
Acaster Malbis
York YO23 2PT
United Kingdom
www.hydro-graphics.co.uk

IDT Systems
The Factory
Dippenhall
Farnham
Surrey GU10 5DW
United Kingdom
www.idt-systems.com

Impressions Foil Ltd
31–32 Shannon Way
Thames Industrial Estate
Canvey Island
Essex SS8 0PD
United Kingdom
www.impressionsfoiling.co.uk

Ineke Hans
INEKEHANS/ARNHEM
Burgemeester Weertsstraat 132
6814 HT Arnhem
The Netherlands
www.inekehans.com

Instrument Glasses
236–38 Alma Road
Ponders End
Enfield EN3 7BB
United Kingdom
www.instrumentglasses.com

K2 Screen
Unit B5, 16–16A Baldwins
Gardens
London EC1N 7RJ
United Kingdom
www.k2screen.co.uk

Luca Cipelletti
AR.CH.IT
Via Pasquale Paoli 8
20143 Milano
Italy
www.ar.ch.it

MadeThought
9 Rathbone Place
London W1T 1HW
United Kingdom
www.madethought.com

Massily Group (UK)
Unit 2, Hendy Industrial Estate
Hendy
Pontarddulais
Swansea SA4 0XP
United Kingdom
www.massilly.com

Modern Activity
19 Warburton Road
London E8 3RT
United Kingdom
www.modernactivity.co.uk

National Glass Centre
Liberty Way
Sunderland SR6 0GL
United Kingdom
www.nationalglasscentre.com

Neil Luxton
Gate House
Stour Valley Business Centre
Sudbury
Suffolk CO10 7GB
United Kingdom
www.neilluxton.co.uk

Polestar
1 Apex Business Park
Boscombe Road
Dunstable
Bedfordshire LU5 4SB
United Kingdom
www.polestar-group.com

Polimoon Packaging
Ellough
Beccles
Suffolk NR34 7TB
United Kingdom
www.polimoon.com

Progress Packaging
The Mill, 150 Penistone Road
Huddersfield HD8 8JQ
United Kingdom
www.progresspackaging.co.uk

Rotor
Rue de Laeken 101
1000 Brussels
Belgium
www.rotordb.org

Royal VKB
PO Box 170
2700 Ad Zoetermeer
The Netherlands
www.royalvkb.com

RS Bookbinders Ltd
Unit 3, Pond Chase Industrial
Estate
Folly Lane, Hockley
Essex SS5 4SR
United Kingdom
www.rsbookbinders.co.uk

Sundolitt Ltd
Suite A2, Stirling Agricultural
Centre, Stirling FK9 4RN
United Kingdom
www.sundolitt.co.uk

Thomas & Vines Ltd
Units 5–6, Sutherland Court
Moor Park Industrial Centre
Tolpits Lane, Watford
Herts WD18 9SP
United Kingdom
www.flocking.co.uk

Vexed Generation
The Grocery
54–56 Kingsland Road
London E2 8DP
United Kingdom
www.vexed.co.uk

VMC Limited
Trafalgar Works
Station Road
Chertsey, Surrey KT16 8BE
United Kingdom
www.vmclimited.co.uk

Wooden Products Ltd
18 Whitting Valley Road
Chesterfield
Derbyshire S41 9EY
United Kingdom
www.woodenproductsltd.com

Zone Creations
64 Windsor Avenue
London SW19 2RR
United Kingdom
www.zone-creations.co.uk

Further Reading

Aav, Marianne (ed.), Elise Kovanen, Marjut Kumela, Helena Leppånen, Susanna Vakkari, Susann Vihma and Tapio Yli-Viikari, *Arabia* (Helsinki: Designmuseo, 2009)

Ambrose, Gavin, and Paul Harris, *Print and Finish* (Lausanne: Ava Publishing, 2006)

Ambrose, Gavin, and Paul Harris, *The Production Manual: A Graphic Design Handbook* (Lausanne: Ava Publishing, 2008)

Ashby, Mike, and Kara Johnson, *Materials and Design: The Art and Science of Material Selection in Product Design* (Oxford and Boston: Butterworth-Heinemann, 2002)

Bann, David, *The All New Print Production Handbook* (Mies: RotoVision and New York: Watson-Guptill Publications, 2006)

Craig, James, *Production for the Graphic Designer* (New York: Watson-Guptill Publications, 1974)

Gatter, Mark, *Getting it Right in Print: Digital Prepress for Graphic Designers* (London: Laurence King Publishing and New York: Harry N. Abrams, Inc., 2005)

Hudson, Jennifer, *Process: 50 Product Designs from Concept to Manufacture* (London: Laurence King Publishing, 2008)

IDTC (International Design Trend Centre), *How Things are Made: Manufacturing Guide for Designer* (Seoul: Agbook, 2003)

Johansson, Kaj, Peter Lundberg and Robert Ryberg, *A Guide to Graphic Print Production*, 2nd edition (Hoboken, N.J.: Wiley, 2007)

Kirkpatrick, Janice, *New Packaging Design* (London: Laurence King Publishing, 2009)

Mason, Daniel, *Materials, Process, Print* (London: Laurence King Publishing, 2007)

Pipes, Alan, *Production for Graphic Designers*, 5th edition (London: Laurence King Publishing and Upper Saddle River: Prentice Hall, 2009)

Thompson, Rob, *Manufacturing Processes for Design Professionals* (London and New York: Thames & Hudson, 2007)

Thompson, Rob, *Product and Furniture Design, The Manufacturing Guides* (London and New York: Thames & Hudson, 2011)

Thompson, Rob, *Prototyping and Low-volume Production, The Manufacturing Guides* (London and New York: Thames & Hudson, 2011)

viction:workshop ltd, *Simply Packaging* (Hong Kong: viction:ary, 2007)

Illustration Credits

Rob and Martin Thompson photographed the processes, materials and products in this book. They would like to acknowledge the following for granting permission to reproduce their photographs and illustrations.

Page 11 (Designersblock brochure): Paul McAnelly at Hawaii Design
Page 13 (Nutcracker): Royal VKB
Page 14 (Screen-printed collection, 'No Sleep Till Hades'): Eleanna Kokkini for Greece is for Lovers
Page 17, left (Pullens' wedding stationery): Campbell Hay
Page 44, left (Bespoke packaging): Simon Farrow at Progress Packaging
Page 46, left (Embossing) and page 47 (all images): Ball Packaging Europe
Pages 60 and 63 (all images): Rotor
Page 66 (Liquid filled pouch): Simon Farrow at Progress Packaging
Page 78, left (Die-cut book): Paul McAnelly at Hawaii Design
Page 84 (Graphics Production title image): Iittala and Arabia
Page 88, right (Zeus): Nikos Alexopoulos for Greece is for Lovers
Page 110, right (Vinyl on perspex): Paul McAnelly at Hawaii Design
Pages 152–55 (all images): Iittala and Arabia
Page 158 (Multiple colour printing): Iittala and Arabia
Pages 160–61 (all images): Iittala and Arabia
Page 182, left (Mario Bellini): Alexander Åhnebrink Design
Page 188, right (Wedding invitations): Campbell Hay
Page 198, right (Folding): Paul McAnelly at Hawaii Design

Acknowledgments

Many individuals and organizations have been extraordinarily generous in providing the technical details found in this book. Their knowledge of processes and materials and their years of hands-on experience have been fundamental in making this book. We should like to thank them for giving up their time and providing amazing insights into the processes that they use and the skills they have developed. We would like to thank Thames & Hudson for their continued support and dedication to producing the highest standard of work.

Rob Thompson: The patience, support and encouragement from family, friends and colleagues has been invaluable throughout. A special thanks to Lina for all her brilliant ideas and advice, and for collecting some really nice packaging examples that we were able to feature in the book. I would also particularly like to thank Martin, my dad, the photographer on the project, who understands how to make beautiful pictures that communicate information better than anyone I know.

Martin Thompson: I would like to thank Rob for the huge compliment of inviting me to work with him on this book. I know first hand the amount of passion and sheer hard work he puts in. Thank you, also, to MDs and machinists alike for all the friendly help I received on the factory visits, and for sharing your skills and expertise. And special thanks to my wife Lynda, Rob's mother, and his brothers for all their patience, wise support and counsel to us both.

Index